ACCIDENTAL
FIRST LADY

On the front lines (and behind the scenes)

of local politics

All attempts have been made to preserve the stories of the events, locales and conversations contained in this collection as the author remembers them. The author reserves the right to have changed the names of individuals and places if necessary and may have changed some identifying characteristics and details such as physical properties, occupations and places of residence in order to maintain their anonymity.

Published by St. Petersburg Press
St. Petersburg, FL
www.stpetersburgpress.com

Design and composition by St. Petersburg Press
Cover design by St. Petersburg Press and Isa Crosta
Cover photo by Scott Keeler, *Tampa Bay Times*, used with permission

Print ISBN: 978-1-940300-46-7
eBook ISBN: 978-1-940300-47-4

First Edition

ACCIDENTAL FIRST LADY

On the front lines (and behind the scenes)

of local politics

By

Kerry Kriseman

For Rick
Our life's journey together has been made richer because
we said yes to a proposition from a friend, over a bottle of wine,
one Sunday evening.

CONTENTS

PREFACE

When I got married in 1992, I thought my new husband would build a career practicing law. I was 24, a St. Petersburg native and recent graduate of the University of South Florida who worked in the marketing department at the *St. Petersburg Times* (now known as the *Tampa Bay Times*). My new life partner, Rick Kriseman, was 30 and just five years into his job at a civil law firm. Life was full, blissful and predictable.

We worked during the week. On weekends, we went out to dinner or a movie. We stayed out until 2 a.m. if we wanted and enjoyed brunch on Sundays.

Two years after our wedding, we bought a remodeled two-bedroom mid-century home in the Lake Pasadena neighborhood in west St. Petersburg. A year later we adopted a yellow Labrador retriever named Abby. We welcomed the birth of our daughter, Jordan, in September 1997, and watched proudly as she took her first, hesitant steps at 15 months.

Then one Sunday evening, a friend who lived nearby asked if he could stop by. Over a bottle of wine – I don't remember if it was red or white – he suggested Rick should run for the St. Petersburg City Council.

That conversation changed the course of our lives. Six years on the City Council led to six years in the state House of Representatives and then two four-year terms as mayor of Florida's fifth largest city. That's eight elections and 22 years in public life for Rick – and for me, the accidental first lady of St. Petersburg.

When I married this lawyer, I could never have imagined the road ahead, and the roles I would be expected to play.

Take the evening I found myself sitting at a dinner between Dan

Rather on my left and my husband on the right. I felt my job was to balance the dinner conversation so that neither man was excluded. I was as nervous as a third grader in the principal's office.

In Cuba, one of Raul Castro's sons greeted me with a firm handshake. I wanted more time with him, but I was left standing outside with my kids as my husband was escorted through thick, hand-carved wooden doors to a private party full of dignitaries and professional athletes.

When Michelle Obama hugged me at a White House holiday party, it felt like a reunion with an old friend.

And I can tell you that Ringo Starr's polite conversation is better than Gene Simmons' bear hug.

Seasoned or novice, male or female, political spouses or partners will see themselves in stories gleaned from my 22 years of political life. Women have always struggled to define themselves amid antiquated societal expectations and misogynistic mores. Running a household and raising children while my husband was away for weeks at a time was challenging and sometimes lonely. While I believe he would do the same for me, my role has been to play the loyal soldier while fighting a "stand by your man" stereotype of a doe-eyed woman gazing up at her husband as he addresses a crowd.

Political spouses may not be on the ballot, but they are in the public eye. Before social media saturated our lives with statements and stories about everything from the mundane to the mind-boggling, I became the subject of a rumor. The faux black fur wrap I wore to a Democratic fundraising dinner was the subject of conversation among a few female political staffers. I was surprised that the women cared more about what I wore than the purpose of the event.

Since 1999, my husband has been elected to something. Throughout eight political campaigns, I've watched him grow into a confident leader. Each campaign launch and governing term was an opportunity for personal growth for both of us. While his was expected, mine was collateral. My experiences as a political spouse have impacted the kind of wife, mother, friend, advocate and community leader I am.

Joyful moments have been juxtaposed with angst-filled days, such as the two Saturdays when our home was ground zero for Black Lives Matter protesters. I've learned to make peace with public life. I've learned to compartmentalize the unavoidable neg-

ativity that is thrust upon politicians. But I'm still human. Sometimes, I internalize the verbal attacks on my husband. It's natural
to want to protect the one you love against hateful rhetoric hurled
by keyboard cowards or people with well-meaning but misguided
intentions.

The year 2020 was troubling for all, some more than others,
and everyone had choices to make. Wear a mask, or not. Speak out
against racial injustice, or not. Search for a middle ground amid
political polarization, or not. The practice of speaking out on behalf
of others, whether it was to protect, advocate or mitigate, separated
leaders from politicians. Still, we have much to learn.

Accidental First Lady shares some of the lessons I've learned
during my 22 years as a political spouse. We are thrust into this
world to help our partners, lovingly supporting them and even
putting their political aspirations ahead of our personal and professional goals. The role is unique and not clearly defined.

Some of us relish this life; others detest it. Some of us are the
introvert to our extrovert spouse. For some, our role is defined the
moment our spouse declares candidacy. For others like me, the
evolution spans the years it takes to raise children.

Political life is unchartered territory for many. Crafting a satisfying but supporting role as a political spouse is like creating a
recipe from scratch. In the 22 years I've been a political spouse,
I've felt amazement, pride, awe, frustration, sadness, elation, anger,
commitment, compassion, and contentment.

The role of political spouse knows no party affiliation. The person whom we love the most has made a choice, hopefully with our
blessing, to dedicate a significant portion of his or her life to public
service. Politicians forsake hefty salaries, personal time and even
their reputations to serve neighbors, friends and fellow citizens.
As their spouses, we serve alongside them.

I hope my stories serve as inspiration and affirmation that life
as an unexpected political spouse can be fulfilling and satisfying.
Politics is partisan, but this book is not. I hope it can serve as a
resource from an unlikely, if not accidental, political spouse who
also became a first lady. I hope my words will show how to survive
and thrive when life's path leads to an unexpected role.

Chapter 1

A CHANCE MEETING

I was 8 years old when I answered a question posed by *Evening Independent* columnist Jim Moorhead. I never envisioned my answer would be a precursor to life as a political spouse.

Each Friday afternoon for several years of childhood, my mother, Ann, packed overnight bags for me and my brother, Steve, and then drove us to Aunt Margaret's fifth-floor apartment in downtown St. Petersburg.

Our parents wanted us to have a Catholic school education, so they both worked two jobs from time to time to pay the tuition. During the week, my dad, Fred Nicolosi, built a pet-products manufacturing business. On weekends, he capitalized on his musical talents, playing the stand-up bass, trumpet, keyboard, and drums at gigs around town. Meanwhile, mom worked as a dental assistant until Friday evenings, when she put on a short cocktail dress and extra makeup and rushed off to wait tables and tend bar at her parents' restaurant, Scully's Square.

Many of Scully's patrons partied until 2 a.m. – much too late for a teenage babysitter to watch Steve and me. The solution was our 74-year-old Aunt Margaret. She relished the role of doting aunt, introducing us to '70s sitcoms like *All in the Family* and *The Jeffersons*. On Saturdays, she gave us money for city bus fare. We learned how to deposit the coins, then take our seats as we rode the few blocks to Webb's City, "The World's Most Unusual Drug Store." Before dinner, we'd play gin rummy. While she cooked, we were kept busy with intellectual challenges, such as crossword puzzles and writing exercises.

One weekend, Aunt Margaret showed me Mr. Moorhead's column in the *Evening Independent*. He invited readers to answer an open-ended question. If he liked your reply, it would be published in a future column. As it happened, Mr. Moorhead lived in my neighborhood, just one block away. I saw him occasionally when I played with his daughters in their third-floor attic, which served as a fort, game room or hideout.

Aunt Margaret was unaware of the connection when she showed me his question: "Where would you like to visit and why?"

In eight years, I'd been to Walt Disney World, camped in Tennessee and visited relatives in Massachusetts. I hadn't taken many trips, but I knew where I'd go if given the choice.

"I want to visit the White House and shake hands with the president," I said. Aunt Margaret guided me as I crafted three paragraphs to submit to the newspaper.

I did not give it another thought until a few weeks later, when Aunt Margaret presented me with the newspaper. There it was, in the lower right half of the page where all of Mr. Moorhead's columns appeared. I must have read it a hundred times after neatly pasting it in my scrapbook, which traveled with me from my childhood home to my first home with Rick. That wish from many years ago sparked an insatiable desire to travel. It also cultivated a greater interest in history and eventually politics.

The summer my parents separated, Dad broke in his new Plymouth Fury by taking my brother and me on a two-week road trip from Florida to Maine. We spent a couple of days in Washington, D.C., visiting the landmarks and Arlington National Cemetery. My dad was a faithful follower of the AAA TripTiks, so he would hand them to me when it was time to find a hotel room for the night. I made sure to pick hotels with a pool, but I also found what I thought might be interesting sights to see.

When I began fifth grade after that road trip in 1977, my class was given an assignment to write a biography on an important American figure. My research paper on President John F. Kennedy, which included a photograph of his grave that I'd taken on a summer road trip with my dad, earned me a perfect score.

In my senior year of high school, I relished a required class called Comparative Political Systems that most of my classmates hated. I excelled in and gravitated toward work that included history, political figures and storytelling.

As a child and teenager, I lived up to the description I read on one of my kindergarten report cards my mother saved. In the comments section, my teacher described me as obedient, quiet and sensitive. When I was older, I overheard Mom telling someone that I was the type of baby who could be put down in the crib and go right to sleep. No fussing or crying. No rocking needed. My infant sleep habits were a glimpse into the type of person I am.

I've been described as affable, accommodating, quiet and unfussy. I'm not a pushover, but I sometimes accommodate others to avoid confrontation. People don't usually see my sense of humor unless they know me well. As the older child, I was content to live in the shadow of my younger, more outgoing brother.

Steve is 14 months younger than me. Irish twins, some would say. I was the epitome of the oldest child. He would agree that I was the better student, although he grew into a talented businessman and an expert at timing stock buys. I did my chores without being asked. He needed a list. My dad used to get annoyed when I would vacuum and dust others' living rooms after the kids I babysat had gone to bed. I craved order and loathed boredom. Since there were no cell phones or cable television to occupy my time, I cleaned.

My brother was selected "Most Humorous" in high school. Although I had many friends and considered myself relatively popular, I was still "Steve's sister." I was comfortable in the background. If required, however, I could hold my own in the spotlight. My ability to easily memorize text and what the nuns called "a good speaking voice" got me drafted for middle school speech competitions.

I graduated from St. Petersburg High School in 1986, the sixth member of the Nicolosi family to be a Green Devil alum. I moved to Pittsburgh that fall to attend Carlow College, a mostly female liberal arts school. The University of Pittsburgh and Carnegie Mellon University were within walking distance, which was convenient for attending fraternity parties and seeing my first boyfriend, a Pitt medical student.

My great aunt, Sister Jane Scully, was president of Carlow from 1966 to 1982 and that helped me get a full scholarship there. Aunt Jane was a trailblazer for women and a mentor to many, including me. As a board member of the Gulf Oil Corp., she pushed for stronger policies on ethics in management. She became the first female member of the Duquesne Club, an elite private club founded in 1873, and we brunched there a few times on Sundays. This former librarian was a hands-on educator who served to influence the next generation.

I should have listened to her when she suggested I pursue a career in communications. I probably would've finished college in four years instead of the six it took while I bounced from business to biology to English before finally choosing mass communications.

I loved Pittsburgh, but Carlow – a small school that emphasized nursing studies – was not a good fit for me. I returned home and attended St. Petersburg Junior College for three years as I sorted through academic and career options. By the time I enrolled at the University of South Florida in Tampa, I was working as a copy clerk in the newsroom of the *St. Petersburg Times*.

No two days in a newsroom are the same. My job as one of a dozen copy clerks was to run news proofs, faxes, and photos from the newsroom to the production floor. Thirty years ago, nothing was digital. If a reporter needed a file on a public figure, I retrieved it from the library. When a page was ready for proofing, I picked it up from the second-floor production department. We worked eight-hour shifts, only sitting for short breaks. I enjoyed watching stories come together in a fast-paced newsroom.

Although I enjoyed my stint in the *Times* newsroom and grew to love the news business, I preferred broadcast over print. Communications and broadcast law classes taught me the history of storytelling over the airwaves. My broadcast news classes were my chance to tell the stories. Sometimes I was in front of the camera. Other times, I hoisted the camcorder on my right shoulder or attached it to the tripod I carried with me when I interviewed newsmakers like the executive director of the S.P.C.A. and mayor of Tampa.

I learned how to ask good questions and write stories that were no longer than 90 seconds. Images from the videotapes were edited to match my words. I couldn't draw a stick figure, but I could film, write and edit a story. Seeing a finished product come together from several pieces gave me a sense of satisfaction. I'd finally found something challenging. Just as Aunt Jane had suggested, it was in the communications field.

One month before I graduated from USF in May 1992, I was offered a full-time job in the *Times'* marketing department. My new job was to write, edit and design the company's internal newspaper, *Times Talk*. At 24, I was the youngest in the department of artists, copy editors and marketing pros. Soon, I joined the dynamic group in creating and writing some of the paper's many advertising campaigns.

My role as *Times Talk* editor required me to interact with staffers from every department, so I kept in touch with my newsroom buddies. If it weren't for them, I might never have met Rick. The sports guys were always up for a round of something after Saturday night deadlines.

It was February 1991. My friend Jennifer, another copy clerk, and I had planned to meet a couple of the guys at Beach Nutts, a new bar on stilts on Sunset Beach. Jen and I headed there first because the guys had another deadline.

Across the wooden deck were two dark-haired men who kept looking our way. One of them seemed to be looking at me. And when they ambled over to chat, he and I realized we recognized each other.

"Do you work at Sun Bank?" he asked.

"Mr. Kriseman?" I replied.

Sun Bank was my other part-time employer during college. Over the months, I had taken notice of the dark-haired customer who went to the farthest drive-thru lane every Friday after 5 p.m. to deposit his paycheck. I confess I was intrigued. I had even looked up his records to see if he had a joint account with a wife. But I did *not* check his bank balance – honest!

Now, the very same Mr. Kriseman was chatting me up. He had been fighting a cold, but his friend dragged him to the bar.

Rick gave me his business card and asked me to call him at my convenience because I worked two jobs and took a full class load. I called on the third day.

We made plans for a Wednesday evening dinner date at Chili's, then a movie. He was leaving for a ski trip two days later and didn't want to wait until his return. I sat at the dining room table at my mom's home, where I still lived, and scanned the movie listings. He asked me to pick, but there were only a few decent choices at Tyrone Square Mall's movie theater. When we tell people our first date was burgers at Chili's followed by *Silence of the Lambs*, we're invariably asked if we enjoyed a nice Chianti afterward, or how did we get to a second date.

It was not an Instagram-worthy evening, but it did begin an intense courtship. That summer, I interned in the newsroom at Fox 13 in Tampa. I worked for free from 9 a.m. to 5 p.m., then raced home in my unairconditioned Honda CRV to shower before Rick picked me up. He often surprised me with a cassette tape of music he'd recorded that I could play on my commutes to Tampa.

We also attended several weddings together that summer, which invited the predictable question of when we would be getting married ourselves. Rick would tell anyone that he knew he wanted to marry me after our first date. If my choice in movies didn't scare him off, I was worried my religion might. He was Jewish and I was Catholic.

If we married, would our children be raised Jewish or Catholic? Because we committed to choosing a religion for our future children, it forced us to truly listen to one another. Rick worried about the transient nature of priests, who are moved from church to church, and the effect it could have on establishing a relationship with one's religious leader. I worried about the possibility of heaven for children who weren't baptized and who didn't believe Jesus to be their savior.

I read books on Judaism, and my family supplied Rick with pamphlets about Catholicism. We met with a priest and a rabbi. We agreed that our children should be raised either Catholic or Jewish, not a combination of both. One of us would have to sacrifice.

I'm not sure if it was evidence of the agreeable personality I displayed in the crib, but I conceded and agreed that our children would be raised Jewish. I could accept the teachings of the Jewish faith without renouncing my beliefs. Rick promised to celebrate Easter and Christmas, the biggest Christian holidays.

My family worried I would forget my religion and that their grandchildren would never sit on Santa's lap. I sensed that my mom worried that having Jewish grandchildren might impact her relationship with them. Rick kept his word. We went to church and celebrated Christian holidays with my family. The hours he spent whittling the trunk of our live Christmas trees, emerging with sappy hands, was proof of his commitment to make our interfaith marriage work.

Both sets of our parents had amicably divorced. I was unsure of the impact that might have on our marriage, since all marriages take work, even those between two people whose parents remained married. But for me, my parents' divorce reinforced my belief that marriages benefit from open and honest communication and the power of positive family relationships.

November 21, 1992, St. Pete Beach, Florida

We'd already negotiated a lot in our marriage by the time our daughter, Jordan, was born in 1997. Six months after parental leave, I left the *Times* to become a full-time, at-home parent. After watching my parents work two jobs and missing my father at dinnertime because he was working late, I was grateful to be able to choose to be home with Jordan and Samuel, who arrived five years after Jordan.

I threw myself into my new role. Every day was a planned activity with Jordan: music on Mondays, story time at the library on Tuesdays, errands on Wednesdays, playgroup on Thursdays, the park on Fridays. When Jordan was just over a year, I joined the Junior League of St. Petersburg. Over time, I chaired five committees and served on the board four times. While Jordan napped, I honed my professional skills, networked with other women, and contributed to the community.

I was content in my roles at home and in the community. It was the perfect balance.

Shortly before Jordan's bedtime one Sunday evening, our friend Lars Hafner called.

"Can I stop by for a minute?" he asked.

— Chapter 2 —

A 22-YEAR
CONVERSATION BEGINS

Sunday evenings are a transitional period when carefree weekends surrender to the anticipation of the week ahead. I don't
remember what we were doing on that Sunday evening in January
1999. It was too early for dinner, but it was already dark. The phone
rang. Rick answered while I helped Jordan, now 16 months old,
practice her newfound walking skills.

"What's up?" I heard the voice say. "Mind if I stop by?" It was our
friend, Lars Hafner.

Lars had a proposition that he wanted to deliver in person. He
lived just five blocks away. Within minutes, he was on our doorstep.

The meeting commenced at our tiny white tile-top kitchen
table. I can't remember whether we were drinking a cabernet or
chardonnay, but I clearly remember the conversation.

Rick and Lars met in 1977 at Boca Ciega High School. Rick was
a freshman, Lars a sophomore. One would later play college basketball at St. Petersburg College, then the University of Buffalo.
The other would be a proud University of Florida Gator who disc
jockeyed for a rock radio station before attending Stetson University College of Law.

Their friendship was cemented on the basketball court. Lars was
a standout on the team, and he was eventually inducted into Boca
Ciega's Hall of Fame. At 5-foot-9, Rick lacked height and, apparently, talent. The basketball coach joked with him that if he ever
tried out for the team again, he would kill him. His determination
to be part of the team eventually won over the coach, who made

him team manager and athletic trainer.

At 25 and 26, these Boca Ciega Pirates teamed up again, this time in politics. The athlete became a legislative candidate who competed for votes instead of baskets. Instead of managing basketball players, Rick handled Lars' platforms, fundraising and strategy as his campaign manager.

Despite a spirited effort by the political novices, Lars lost to a longtime incumbent, State Representative Dottie Sample. In a rematch two years later, Lars won. Rick credited the win to Lars having a new campaign manager. Lars served in the state House for 12 years. Term limits forced him out, but he kept his hand in local politics.

"How about you run for City Council?" Lars asked Rick. The proposal jarred us out of our light buzz. We were in our sixth year of marriage and had known each other almost eight years, but this subject had never come up.

Rick had never uttered a word about pursuing political office. The most memorable thing about President Clinton's 1992 win was my mom naming the stray cats that showed up on her doorstep Bill and Al. Besides a perfect voting record, my only political involvement was a campaign volunteer stint for state Sen. Jeanne Malchon.

"Why not?" urged Lars. Incumbent Bob Kersteen had held the City Council seat for some time, and while he was a decent member, Lars felt it was time for fresh blood and new ideas. Lars said that Rick was the ideal candidate to inject energy into city politics and challenge the status quo. We were surprised, intrigued and flattered. But mostly, we were unsure.

We said good night to Lars, and we promised to mull over the proposition. Sometimes, ideas become reality only after someone else plants the seed. A few days and several discussions later, we said yes. As Lars had said, "Why not?"

Personal injury attorneys are often called ambulance chasers because of their reputation for capitalizing on accident victims' injuries. It was true that Rick did represent people who were injured in auto accidents that were someone else's fault. He wasn't getting rich off their injuries. He took phone calls after hours. He reduced his fees if a settlement didn't net enough money to pay a client's medical bills. His clients weren't just his livelihood. He was helping them put their lives back together.

If elected to the City Council, Rick could use his skills of empathetic listening and connecting with people to serve his constituents. His lawyerly critical thinking skills and attention to detail would come in handy when researching and understanding issues that would come before the council. I knew that if he had the chance to serve, he would do so with the same empathy and expertise he employed in his law practice. There was no good reason to say no to running.

The time from "yes" to election day passed swiftly. January to March is a cruelly short amount of time to craft a platform, raise money, engage voters, design marketing collateral, and establish name recognition. There was no honeymoon phase for this campaign. Our strategy was "learn as you go." Thankfully, we had a few trusted advisors, friends who became volunteers, and loyal family members who believed in Rick.

Many spouses are not suited for working together. For some, it might be too much time together. Others clash on the fundamentals of running a business. Some couples find it hard to leave work at the office. Being married to your business partner can jeopardize a marriage.

It was different for Rick and me.

In 1994, budget cuts at the *St. Petersburg Times* meant that my marketing job was reduced from full time to part time. I had spare time, no kids yet, and a desire to be productive.

That same year, Rick left his law firm to open a solo practice. As a new business owner and sole practitioner, it was necessary to keep overhead low. Managing Rick's law office became my new part-time job. I was an easy hire. I had the time and a vested interest in the success of the business, and I did not need to be vetted or paid.

My stint at the law office ended with the 1997 birth of our daughter, Jordan, when we agreed that I should become an at-home parent. Two years later, when Rick agreed to run for the City Council, I was happy to become his co-worker again. We always enjoyed working together for a common purpose. Serving the citizens of St. Petersburg would be an honor.

The three years I worked with Rick at the law office taught me things about him that I might not have learned otherwise. We had separate offices, but the doors between our spaces remained open except when he was with clients. He spoke to every client with the same kindness he showed me. He listened. He consoled. He reassured.

His patience and willingness to listen are now his strongest and most-admired traits as a politician. Politics is ugly at times. Most of the time, the focus is on the negativity, partisanship, bickering and backstabbing. When I tell others that my husband is a politician, I sometimes do so hesitantly and apologetically. I usually follow it with, "He's one of the good ones."

Simply put, Rick's passion for politics is driven by a desire to help others. As his wife, I have had a front row seat for 22 years of politics. I've learned that there is no instruction manual for how to be a political spouse. Fortunately for us, Rick's first political campaign was as local as it gets. Running a campaign was like on-the-job training.

One week after Rick said yes to Lars' proposal, about 30 friends and family came to our 1,400-square-foot home for a $25-a-head wine and cheese fundraiser. Rick had little to no name recognition outside our family and friends, so they were our first supporters.

What he lacked in name recognition, he made up for with hustle. Rick spent the roughly two months of hard campaigning convincing as many people as possible that they should vote for him. I rolled with the punches as Rick spent most weeknights attending neighborhood meetings, community events and forums. With no advertising budget, it was the only way he could share his platform and humbly ask for votes.

My evenings were spent reading, rocking, then gently laying a sleeping Jordan down in her crib before I got to work folding and stuffing fundraising letters into envelopes.

It seemed as if we had just finished that bottle of wine with Lars when election day arrived. The first-time candidate with virtually no name recognition, budget or viability hoped to be elected the next City Council member for District 1.

A meager budget meant that the election night party was in the same spot as the kickoff: our living room. I didn't even buy celebratory Champagne. We were political novices.

Our short but thrilling roller coaster ride of a campaign came to an abrupt halt. Winning was a long shot, and Rick took the loss in stride. As a political newcomer, he earned a respectable 42% of the vote. We Monday-morning-quarterbacked the what ifs? What if there had been more time, money or a few more endorsements? We did not feel defeated, only grateful for the experience. It was an almost insurmountable feat to win a 60-day campaign as a political newcomer against an incumbent.

The ride was over. Relief and exhaustion set in as we looked back on the last two months. Campaigns can feel like marathons. This first one was like a sprint. We returned to watching sitcoms on the sofa at night instead of attending forums and stuffing envelopes. Rick vowed to stay involved in city government. Soon, he was appointed to the city's Nuisance Abatement Board. He got to know Mayor David Fischer and other council members. He learned how city government works.

Life resumed to normalcy, but not for long. Kersteen resigned his seat the next year to run for the state House. Rick's talent for connecting with people and his commitment to stay involved earned praise from the city's politicians. In March 2000 he was appointed to fill the seat vacated by the man who beat him the year before.

Early political life was low-key. The media doesn't pay much attention to the actions or politics of City Council members. As a family, we were relatively anonymous except for the times we attended city events and our presence was announced.

With his appointment to the council, it was clear Rick had found his calling as a politician, even if I wasn't ready to admit it.

Our lives were about to change.

Rick and his dad, Danny Kriseman – City Council Swearing In - 2001

Chapter 3

LEARNING CURVE

A first-time visitor to St. Petersburg might be surprised to learn that the hip, thriving city was once the punch line in jokes about boredom, benches and old people.

The town got its start in 1888, when a Russian-born railroad promoter named Pyotr Alexeyevitch Dementyev brought the Orange Belt Railway down the Pinellas peninsula to a tiny settlement whose predominant landowner was John C. Williams, a gentleman farmer from Michigan.

Local legend has it that they flipped a coin for the right to name the place. Dementyev (who had changed his name to Peter Demens) won and chose the name St. Petersburg, for the city in his native country. Williams' consolation prize was the right to name the tiny community's new hotel. He called it the Detroit, after his hometown in Michigan.

Over the next century, St. Petersburg grew in fits and starts. A real estate boom in the Roaring '20s fueled a growth spurt and so did World War II. Thousands of soldiers who lived and trained in the area during the war came back to make their homes in the place that called itself "The Sunshine City."

But a city that enjoyed sunshine an average of 361 days a year could not shake its reputation as "God's waiting room," a rigidly segregated place where hordes of listless seniors sat on green benches (white people only, of course) amid hordes of pigeons.

"The old people sit, passengers in a motionless streetcar without destination," *Holiday* magazine reported in 1958.

How things have changed!

Now St. Pete is a hip, diverse, trendy destination for millennials, tourists and beautiful people. It is known as a city of the arts, with must-see museums, including the Dali Museum, that attract

tourists of all ages. Walk down bustling Beach Drive and you can
hear a multitude of languages. It seems as if everyone wants to be
in St. Pete.

The city is renowned for its quality of life. People from all over
the world come to play on its beach and bay, rent bikes to explore
neighborhoods, eat at trendy restaurants, catch a Major League
Baseball game in an air-conditioned stadium, or attend a Grand
Prix auto race. Many decide to call it home.

St. Petersburg is a progressive city where diverse ideas are welcome, the kind of place where dreams can become reality. Some
call the city "Silicon Shores," a play on San Francisco's Silicon Val-
ley, Seattle's Silicon Forest, and Denver's Silicon Mountain tech
communities. Steady growth has resulted in an attractive real estate
market and a ripe climate for business startups.

Where St. Pete started and where it was going was part of the reason Rick decided to make that two-month whirlwind City Council
run in 1999. The idea that he might contribute to a resurgent city
lit a fire in him. Despite losing that 1999 campaign, he vowed to
stay involved in city government.

Relationships often breed success. Sometimes it is who you
know. He got to know everyone at City Hall, including the mayor
and the other council members. He maintained a relationship of
mutual respect with the man who beat him. Because there were
still two years left in the term for the seat Rick was appointed to
after his former opponent resigned to run for the state House, Rick
had to run again in 2001 to earn the right to serve those two years.

Crews from two local televisions stations camped out in our
living room until the election was called in Rick's favor. I kept re-
plenishing the buffet spread of catered Italian food and managed
to persuade our daughter to wear the dress I'd picked out for the
evening instead of the Minnie Mouse costume she preferred.

Those two years passed quickly, and in 2003, Rick ran and was
elected again. Our election night guest list had outgrown our living
room, so we celebrated at Saffron's, a Jamaican restaurant known
for its jerk chicken.

Rick was a City Council member during the infancy of St. Pete's
renaissance. The rebirth included new businesses, an expanding
arts scene that garnered national attention, and a fancy two-sto-
ry shopping center and movie theater complex in the middle of
downtown.

Serving on the council was like being part of an extended family. The mayor's kids were close in age to Jordan, and so were the children of other council members. It wasn't only the council members who attended parades and park openings. The families congregated. The children played. Sometimes we even broke bread together. City politics were unsullied by division and partisanship. We knew who the Democrats and Republicans were, but it didn't matter. We liked each other. It was a wonderful indoctrination into political life.

Throughout his six-year tenure, Rick established a reputation for tenacity tempered with thoughtfulness. He thoroughly read every page in the pile of documents distributed to members before meetings. Lawyerly instincts guided his principled conduct.

His thoroughness sometimes created headaches when the mayor spent weeks lobbying for certain issues, hoping the votes would come swiftly and in his favor. Rick wasn't being difficult. He employed the same kind of passionate advocacy as a council member that he did when representing auto accident victims.

He represented District 1, the westernmost part of St. Pete, but like all council members, he served citywide. He continued to run his law office, taking off Thursdays for council meetings. In the evenings, he boned up on the issues that were pending before the council. He was working two jobs while I was taking care of Jordan and the house.

Rick was a devoted father and helpful husband, but his growing love affair with politics required me to adapt. Some spouses might've resented their husband being out a few evenings a week, or spending hours poring over documents instead of spending time with them. Watching my husband serve our city made it hard for me to be selfish. He loved what he was doing. And he was making a difference. How could I ask him to stop, just so he could spend more evenings with me watching television?

There was never a division of labor in our marriage based on societal mores and stereotypical expectations of men and women. I never took for granted that it was a luxury for me to have the choice to stay home with our children until they started kindergarten. It was natural for me to assume more duties at home while Rick worked two jobs. I'd worked since I was a teenager. In college, I worked two jobs to pay for my car and insurance. I contributed to the household while I attended college locally. Stay-at-home parent was now my job.

I created a schedule of stimulating and socially engaging activities for Jordan that kept both of us busy. When she napped, I made a cup of coffee, grabbed a granola bar, and headed to the computer, where I worked on Junior League tasks or designed the Temple Beth-El monthly newsletter. As a former professional, it was important to keep my skills current while contributing to our community.

When Jordan was 5, we adopted Samuel. Shortly before her sixth birthday, she started kindergarten. I started over with Samuel. Monday music, Tuesday story time, Wednesday playdates, Thursday gymnastics....

Life was humming along. Occasionally, Rick's City Council duties meant that we'd climb on top of the back of a convertible to ride down Central Avenue and Beach Drive for the annual Festival of States and Santa parades. Twice, we accompanied Rick to Washington, D.C., when the City Council lobbied federal lawmakers. We always went in March, when it was bitterly cold and windy. Rick would spend the day on Capitol Hill. I'd bundle up the kids, board the Metro and visit Smithsonian museums, the National Zoo and the monuments.

Festival of States Parade – City Council - 2005

In six years, there were only a handful of controversial moments. St. Pete was a relatively big city, but at times, it had retained a small-town Mayberry mentality. Growth was encouraged, but mostly in downtown. I learned the meaning of the acronym, NIMBY. The "Not in My Backyard" crowd embraced new projects, so long as they weren't in their neighborhood.

In 2004, the cozy branch library where I spent most Tuesday mornings with the children became the focus of a NIMBY dispute. The city's public library system and the mayor wanted to close the Azalea Branch Library and merge it with a new, larger library on a campus of St. Petersburg College.

Both buildings were in Rick's district, which meant that many of the questions and criticisms were directed at him. Opponents of the proposal believed their beloved little library was being stolen. They refused to see what they would gain: a larger, technologically advanced space where kids could learn and grow. There would even be a playground outside the library and an expanded catalog of books.

Rick, who favored the proposal, attended numerous neighborhood meetings to stress the pros and listen to the cons. Some of the opponents seemed to forget how to respectfully disagree. One of them even accused Rick of having an affair with the college president's wife. Surely sexual impropriety must have something to do with his support of the new library!

Rick was accustomed to the give-and-take of public office, but this issue – which consumed much of the year – was a first for me. Women who I thought didn't know or care that my husband was on the City Council suddenly sought me out.

One mom, whom I frequently saw at the grocery store, told me that a new library on the college campus might endanger young children. College students and children should not share the same space, she declared. Had she inspected the library plans, she would have seen that the children's section of the new library would be well staffed and quartered off with sea creature cutouts. The seats would be too small for college students. Her argument was flawed, but I didn't tell her that. I just smiled politely and promised to relay her concerns to Rick.

Another critic was the younger sister of one of Rick's childhood friends. She was one of the handful of people who attended Rick's first campaign fundraiser, and she had told me about Tuesday story time at the Azalea library and introduced me to Mother Goose, the librarian who conducted it each week. One afternoon during nap time, she called to let me know she was going to speak out against the library proposal when Rick addressed it at her neighborhood association meeting. But this would not affect our friendship, she said.

I was surprised, but not offended, that she disagreed with Rick. I thanked her for letting me know, then changed the subject. Later, she was true to her word. At the neighborhood meeting, she spoke honestly and respectfully to Rick. Our friendship remained unchanged.

I had survived my first political controversy with a friend. Respect for civil discourse and the ability to disagree without being disagreeable preserved our friendship, even if it didn't save the Azalea Branch Library.

Rick was becoming known as a leader who spoke out even when his stand on an issue was unpopular. An early moment that stands out was his deciding vote to put the money from the city's sale of Weeki Wachee Springs into a fund that the city could use on parks, recreation, beautification and preservation.

When Halloween decorations on a citizen's private property were deemed racist, and then destroyed, by a fringe political group, Rick was the only council member to demand answers from a complacent mayor and police chief. He wanted to know why a St. Petersburg police officer sat in his patrol car and watched as members of the Uhurus, the African People's Socialist Party, destroyed a hanged effigy of Frankenstein, which they contended was based on a "history of hanging African people." The Uhurus bullied and harassed private citizens and elected officials in the name of equal rights and reparations for Africans. Some leaders preferred to ignore their illegal actions rather than hold them accountable. The police chief feared retaliation and riots like the ones that rocked the city for days in 1996 after a Black man was killed by a white police officer who said he was defending himself. Rick publicly pressed for accountability and an investigation as to why the officer watched the Uhurus trespass and destroy property.

The *St. Petersburg Times* aggressively covered this issue, which seemed to anger the Uhurus. Flyers depicting Rick with a noose around his neck were plastered on street corners. Rick wasn't deterred. I was busy taking care of two little ones, and at first, I didn't make the connection that the anger behind the flyers was a threat to Rick and our family. The picture of Rick in a noose was a message for him to back down, or else. I was grateful our kids were too young to read the paper.

I could've told their leader, Omali Yeshitela, that their outrage was in vain. I would've told Yeshitela that Rick once stood in front of a client's running vehicle after he tried to steal a settlement check. Standing up to the Uhurus wasn't up for debate. Rick felt they should have been held accountable for vandalizing private property. Even if it meant threats.

If our lives were going to change because Rick found a passion for public service, then it was going to be worth it. Rick would serve boldly, and I would support and defend him when it was called for. Our lives might've been easier if he chose to serve quietly, but he wouldn't be serving his truth. Rick's refusal to fade into the background earned him the role of City Council chair in 2005. I wasn't yet referring to myself as a political spouse, but I was proud to be married to a man who showed up, stood up and spoke out.

Under St. Pete's strong mayor form of government, Rick served in the shadow of the mayor. He knew the scope of job he was elected to do, and he respected the boundaries. The City Council years were an initiation into politics. Our marriage was tested when roles changed. We managed to navigate infertility and loss as we strived to complete our family. In fact, it was the mayor and his wife who recommended the adoption agency that helped us welcome Samuel in November 2002. In January 2004, Samuel stole the show while Rick held him on his left hip, right hand on the Torah, to be sworn in for what would be a final City Council term.

In less than two years, Rick would ascend a bigger stage, adding a second ZIP code to his address.

— Chapter 4 —

SMILE, WALK, REPEAT

My kids looked perfect in the outfits I'd chosen. But I still worried whether they met the expectations of the media consultant who'd issued the directive. I debated with myself over Jordan's dress color and whether I should style her hair in a half-up, half-down style or in pig tails.

Longtime Floridians know that August is the hottest month of a nearly year-round summer season. We were instructed to arrive at 2 p.m., right in the middle of Samuel's usual afternoon nap time. He was only 3, and the second half of our days and peaceful dinners were predicated on whether he had his nap.

I knew I'd need to be patient with the kids if we were to survive hours of filming in the sweltering heat. I packed a cooler with water bottles and snacks. They were as perfectly curated as their outfits. Only clean snacks of Gummy bears, apple slices and Goldfish made the cut.

Bill Fletcher was one half of the media team from Nashville that Rick's campaign hired to produce commercials when Rick decided to seek a seat in the Florida House of Representatives in 2006. With more than 500 campaigns under their belt, Bill and his business partner, John Rowley, were experts at crafting compelling messages that tell a candidate's story without making it seem like a political ad.

I didn't know Bill, but he greeted me with a hug as I stepped out of our minivan with the kids. His friendly Nashville drawl endeared him to the kids, as he enveloped their small hands inside his with firm handshakes.

I'd been through three City Council campaigns with Rick, but we'd never done a commercial. He'd served the citizens of St. Pete for six years, but he needed to introduce himself again, to a bigger audience.

With each political race, it seemed like the bar was raised. Incumbency is a benefit, but the candidate's history of votes and positions on issues come into play. There is something to be said for being a newcomer, if not the underdog, in a political race. There's no history to defend. People haven't yet met you, or your family. After six years on the council, many people knew Rick. He'd built a reputation as a thoughtful but thorough public servant, a fighter who was a leader among his peers. He hoped to use those attributes as a state House representative. It was time to introduce Rick to the people he hoped to serve in west St. Petersburg and the nearby communities of Gulfport, Lealman, Pinellas Park and Kenneth City.

A commercial would tell voters what kind of legislator he would be and show who he was as a husband and father.

The homeowners who offered their picturesque front porch for the shoot were kind enough to let the media team set up a makeshift makeup studio inside. We recruited our friends Mike and Natalya and their daughters Rehna and Elizabeth to pose as our neighbors. Crew members offered water and comfortable seats. Jodi the makeup artist and I became fast friends when she exclaimed, "Well I don't need to do much" after inspecting my makeup job. My face was her canvas, and she was a talented artist. I wished I could recreate how she emphasized my eyes. They looked brighter and less tired. I didn't want to wash my face that evening. It was as if she'd placed a beautiful bow on a nicely wrapped present. Could she come live with us and do this for me every day, I joked?

I hadn't been on television since I was 5. My mom was a field trip driver when our kindergarten class visited the set of *Romper Room*, a children's television show that ran from 1965 to 1980. Miss June was the host who called each child by name. I see so and so over here, and so and so over there, she would say. It took a lot of coaxing from my mom and teacher to get me to join my classmates on the set.

The idea of being on camera made me a little nervous, but I told myself I wouldn't be doing this alone. I figured anyone who watched the ad would be focused on Jordan and Samuel. I was determined to enjoy what I thought would be a once-in-a-lifetime opportunity to appear on television with my family.

Aside from our wedding video and family movies, the only times

I appeared on camera were for my college news reporting and broadcast production classes, to be seen only by my professors. That was 14 years ago. The summer before my senior year of college, I worked fulltime at an unpaid internship at WTVT in Tampa. The videographers loved to teach, and they didn't mind staying a few minutes at a scene to let me practice a standup on camera while the reporter was writing the story in the van. The videographers were also editors, and they let me sit in the compact editing bays in the studio. I closely watched as they furiously spliced and blended images and sound in time for the 6 p.m. news. Later that summer, it was often my hands that turned the large black dials left and right, cutting unnecessary images and preserving the best footage. I learned that the camera wasn't something to fear, whether I was in front of it or behind.

After graduation, I accepted a position in the *St. Petersburg Times* marketing department as a writer, designer and editor. I wasn't using the broadcast news degree that took six years to earn, but I enjoyed the work. Occasionally, I wound up in ads for the newspaper's promotional campaigns.

We were a team of six who created, produced and executed promotional campaigns. Our mission was to attract readers with contests that would entice them to keep buying the paper, increasing their chances of winning. Most of us were in our 20s and early 30s, the ideal demographic for these contests. We were ideal, ready-made models – on site, willing and free.

Our spouses were sometimes tapped to appear in the ads. Rick cheerfully posed with my co-workers and me next to a large dumpster to promote a recycling campaign. Our newlywed status earned us the role of Valentine's Day couple for a love-themed conteSt. Sometimes it was only my hands they wanted. My long and slender fingers with manicured nails made me the resident hand model.

Now, the feeling of being part of something creative that could help Rick win an election produced a familiar rush of adrenaline.

I remembered all of this when I got nervous the night before the shoot. I reminded myself that I'd filmed and been filmed many times. This time the stakes were higher. My husband was a candidate in a competitive political race. This wasn't practice, like my internship. Nor was it for a newspaper that would be thrown out or recycled the next day. This political commercial would be seen on cable and network television channels several times a day for two months.

Unless you own your own business, chances are you're never going to film a commercial with your family. Preparation quelled my nerves. I brought backup clothes. Two extra outfits for the kids, three white dress shirts for Rick, a second top for me. Snacks, books, Legos and Matchbox cars kept Jordan and Samuel occupied between takes.

Deciding how to dress the kids was easy. Dressing myself was harder. Many of the political wives I saw in photographs and on television wore suits. I hated suits. I never wore them. Not even when I worked as a bank teller and panty hose were part of the dress code.

The idea that we would be on television for weeks made me question every outfit idea I had. I wasn't instructed to wear church clothes, but no one gave me guidance. I assumed the professionals figured I would know exactly what to wear.

But I didn't.

The only thing I knew for certain was that I didn't want my outfit to offend or distract. Thousands of voters would see this commercial. It was Rick's name on the ballot, but the kids and I could be viewed as a liability or an asset. It's the candidates who are seen and heard the moSt. But I believed that most voters were curious about the people who live with the candidate. I wanted to make a good impression. I was now on a bigger stage, too.

I needed to appear conservative yet not stuffy. I needed to look like myself to those who knew me. A buttoned-up suit and pumps were not part of my repertoire. Whatever I wore needed to hide the inevitable perspiration from the midday sun.

I knew I couldn't wear what I really felt like wearing, my stay-at-home mom uniform of shorts, casual top and sandals. I settled on a high-waisted asymmetrical blue denim skirt paired with a satin, lightweight black and white wrap top. Feminine and conservative, yet not too casual to raise any eyebrows. The three-inch wedge tan sandals I chose were comfortable and sturdy enough to navigate the hexagon sidewalks that we walked for what seemed like a hundred times, always smiling at the camera.

Samuel's sweaty hands kept slipping out of mine as we walked toward the camera over and over for two hours. A couple of times, we ducked inside a nearby bungalow for water breaks and to cool off in the icy cold air conditioning. Jodi the makeup artist blotted perspiration and reapplied foundation and powder that had melted off. Refreshed and hydrated, we'd head back to the sidewalk until the crew was satisfied that they'd captured enough footage to take back to Nashville.

John Rowley and Bill Fletcher – Fletcher, Rowley, Chao, Riddle

Each time the commercial aired, our phone rang. Friends and family loved it. I realized I had taken for granted how great the kids performed that day. Samuel was 3 and Jordan was 7. They took direction from adults they'd never met. They were tired and hot, but they never complained. I know their presence in the commercial helped endear Rick to voters.

People we never met told us how to walk, whose hand to hold, and how many times to do it. They combed our hair, made us look prettier and less shiny. Once the outfits were chosen, I relaxed and had a good time. The broadcast news major in me enjoyed talking to Bill and his crew about the filming process. They told me why they chose the Kenwood neighborhood for this shoot. The bungalow house was nice but not flashy. The nearby park gave them access to a second location without having to pack up the equipment and travel to a new set. I understood why they wanted us to walk the same steps with the same smiles on our faces for what seemed like a hundred times. It was important to get the best shots. If they needed to return to St. Pete to reshoot, that meant more money the campaign would need to spend that could be utilized elsewhere. Bill even let Jordan and Samuel watch through the camera lens as they shot video of their father.

If you're a political spouse, chances are you'll appear in at least one commercial. Preparation and confidence are underrated. Knowing what to wear, where you need to be, and what you'll be doing or saying let you relax and enjoy the process. I let go of the fear of how we'd be perceived on television.

Now, I enjoyed seeing our family on television. So did the kids. We could recite Rick's script from memory.

Political commercials can be more than a vehicle on a path to victory. In our case, they're snapshots of pivotal moments in Rick's political life and ours as a family. A keepsake for sure.

Candidates don't win elections alone. It may be their name on the ballot, but a collaborative team effort gets them to the finish line. That includes the spouse and children. The goal to win must transcend the candidate. Everyone who is part of the campaign must be committed to their job. My job has always been to support, advise and join the team in talking with voters and convincing them that Rick deserves their support.

One day, there will be no more politics. No one will ask us to be in a commercial. Memories of that day became part of our family's history. I knew it was important to cherish these moments. It was one more step toward adapting to the changes that would soon come as Rick's political career grew.

John Rowley and Bill Fletcher – Fletcher, Rowley, Chao, Riddle

— Chapter 5 —

A BIGGER STAGE AND A
CHANGE OF ADDRESS

C hess players will tell you that their game is more challenging than checkers. Both games require calculated moves. Good players are strategic. They possess precise timing. They learn their opponent's weaknesses. Innate or learned, instincts tell the players when to make their moves.

Politics can be like chess. Every move brings risk. Well-calculated and data-driven moves usually equal victory. Carelessness and haughtiness often guarantee loss.

Rick taught Samuel to play chess, with both hovering over the board as they plotted moves. Rick almost always won. That's the benefit of experience. But he showed Samuel how patience and careful thinking, combined with ferocious competitiveness, lead to victory.

Rick's instinct and timing led him to run for an open seat in the Florida House of Representatives midway through his third term on the City Council. The decision to seek higher office and serve in the state capital of Tallahassee was as casual as the few clicks it takes to spend hundreds of dollars on Amazon Prime. It was like boarding a train to an unknown destination, but I wanted to support his passion for service.

Partisanship was rarely an issue during the mostly congenial City Council years. But now, for the first time, Rick was on the ballot as a Democrat. If he won, he would serve in a chamber where Republicans enjoyed an advantage of more than 2 to 1. Rick had never backed down from a challenge. In early 2006, he declared his candidacy for the state House seat serving west St. Pete, where we lived, and parts of Gulfport, Kenneth City, Lealman and Pinellas Park.

The leap to a bigger stage didn't faze Jordan, now 8, and Samuel, almost 4. I kept our home humming while Rick campaigned. Friends and family were invaluable in the early years of his political career, but they weren't political operatives. For the first time, Rick had a campaign manager, treasurer and media team that wasn't him, me, family or friends.

When I wasn't driving 16 miles round trip twice a day to take Jordan and Samuel to school, I was cleaning the house, cooking the meals and walking our dogs, driving Jordan to dance, and reading to Samuel before bed.

Rick's campaign schedule was busier than any City Council race. He spent weekends and weeknights walking neighborhoods. On doorsteps and on the phone, he introduced himself to voters, discussed his platform and asked for support. By day, he represented auto accident victims. At night, he attended neighborhood meetings, candidate forums and debates.

I adjusted my expectations on how much I would see Rick and how often we would eat dinner as a family. Sometimes I joined Rick in distributing campaign literature. Some nights, I headed to campaign headquarters to call voters. I'd read from a prepared script but ended up adlibbing the more calls I made. Voters seemed to like hearing from the candidate's spouse. Swaying votes made me feel like I was contributing to the race instead of simply tending to the home and children.

Rick won with 64% of the vote. In a few short months, he would be headed to Tallahassee. But first we had to be in the capital the Tuesday before Thanksgiving for the swearing-in of new legislators and the House speaker. We were on a swift, exciting track toward the next phase of our political life.

Rick's dad died in 2003, before Rick was elected to his final term on the council. His mother lived in a nursing home in Atlanta. I know it meant a lot to him to have my mom, aunt and 17-year-old cousin join us in Tallahassee for the ceremony.

Our eagerness to make the 300-mile journey north into a mini-vacation dictated the route we chose. We would take the scenic route.

U.S. 19 connects the Gulf of Mexico with Lake Erie. It's one of

Florida's oldest north-south roads. It reached the state in 1929, long before the first interstate. Speed limits range from 30 to 70. Accelerate, decelerate, watch the rearview window for flashing lights. It was worth it for us to show the kids some sites that weren't Disney.

Our Toyota Sienna's cruise control got a workout as we passed through towns like Homosassa, which attracts tourists who come to swim with the manatees in near-constant 72-degree water. Soon, we ascended a two-lane overpass through Crystal River, home to the CR-3 Nuclear Power Plant. I pointed out the reactors to Jordan and Samuel as if they were national landmarks.

Rhythmic speed fluctuations and small-town roads that transitioned to highways before coasting into one hamlet after another were the drumbeats of our journey.

I chuckled as we drove past the exit for Frostproof, certainly an accurate Florida moniker. Did an abundance of otters live in Otter Creek, where the last census counted just 121 residents?

What did Red Level mean? We were far from Georgia, a state known for its red clay. I later learned that Cross City birthed three professional athletes: Nick Collins of the Green Bay Packers, Duke Dawson of the New England Patriots and Eugene McDowell, a former University of Florida basketball player and third-round pick in the 1985 NBA draft.

The Suwannee River runs through Fanning Springs, which inspired a (thankfully) brief rendition from Rick and me of "Way Down Upon the Suwannee River!" The state song, written by Stephen Foster in 1851, was originally titled "Old Folks at Home." It was a minstrel song, written in the dialect of slaves, and throughout the years was increasingly criticized for romanticizing plantations and slavery. Thankfully, many of the lyrics were changed and it's no longer the *only* choice of historical songs performed at gubernatorial inaugurations.

Perry was the last "big city" before the final stretch to Tallahassee. The hilly swath of road meandered past farms bordered with white fences. Stately homes stood at attention in the distance. We coasted down the last hill before Highway 27 became Apalachee Parkway. In the distance was the Capitol, a tall, white pillar that stretched to the sky.

We checked into the Marriott, swiped the room key, and unpacked. Vacation mode surrendered to anticipation. The next morning Rick would be sworn in as a state legislator. An infectious buzz permeated the hotel hallways as we passed other families. We smiled and said hello, as if we were all guests invited to the same party. I wondered if they were hiding their nervousness and excitement, too.

Swearing-in day at the Capitol was crowded with families and well-wishers. Toddlers to teens tagged along with their parents in the rush to find their seats. There were so many babies. Our kids hadn't been babies that long ago. I remembered how exhausting those early days with infants can be. My life would be changing, but at least my kids were somewhat independent and slept through the night.

People I'd never met seemed to know Rick. They congratulated each other and exchanged back slaps, those half-hugs between men trying to avoid an all-out embrace. I was introduced to countless people, but I could only recall a few names. We held on tight to Jordan and Samuel, leading them through the narrow maze of white-walled hallways adorned with black and white photographs depicting images of Florida history.

Winding through the Capitol hallways left me dizzy. We found my mom, Aunt Marcia (who we called Amy because that's all I could say when I was a toddler) and cousin, Shella. They would sit in the gallery with Jordan and Samuel while I joined Rick on the House floor.

Mom and Amy – State House swearing in The Florida Capitol,
Tallahassee, Florida, - 2006

After passing through what felt like a secret underground tunnel, we emerged in a different section of the Capitol. It was like opening the airplane window after landing. This part of the Capitol looked and felt different. We whizzed past offices, including then-Gov. Jeb Bush's, before checking out Rick's new digs.

Swearing-in day is a production. I tried to take it all in, but it felt like swimming against a current. We waded through swarms of lawmakers, legislative staffers, lobbyists and families as we ventured to the elevator that would send the kids with my mom to the gallery. Rick and I would follow the rest of the legislators and their spouses to the House floor.

Rep. Kriseman – State House swearing in - 2006

We found Rick's desk, near the back of the room. The House floor was not the place to be if you detested crowds. I was immediately regretful when I saw the huge bouquet of congratulatory flowers sitting on Rick's desk. They were from the political parties, lobbyists and other favor seekers. There should've been a bouquet from the kids and me. Each swearing-in and beginning of session thereafter, I made sure a big spray from Blossoms on Monroe Street was on his desk.

We sat at the too-tiny-for-two desk while other House members – Democrat and Republican - approached and introduced themselves with hugs and small talk. Marco Rubio, now a U.S. senator, was speaker then. As the youngest speaker in Florida's history spoke, I wondered what he and Rick might have in common.

Opposite political ideologies didn't prevent Rick and him from establishing a rapport. Rick appreciated Rubio's sense of humor, which can be an asset when debates become raucous. Back then, Rubio understood that relationships are nurtured when colleagues can mingle socially. The congeniality legislators shared over a meal was often absent in committee meetings and on the House floor.

As soon as Speaker Rubio pounded the gavel, I heard, "Mama, Mama, Mama!" I looked up to my left to the gallery and made eye contact with my mom, who was holding Samuel. His arms were outstretched. He was almost 4 and often refused to hold my hand in public. Independent and strong, his arms were outstretched. Face red and wet with tears, he was trying to reach me. I looked around, figuring everyone else could hear him, too.

My mom held Samuel up. She thought if he could see us, he might calm down. But that only infuriated him. The cocktail of crowds, noise and activity had taken its toll.

I considered leaving the House floor to get to him in the gallery. I knew I wouldn't be able to find my way through the halls that reminded me of a fall festival corn maze. I didn't even know which elevator would take me to the gallery. I had no credentials, so the security guards probably wouldn't have let me re-enter the House floor. I didn't want to miss being there when Rick was sworn in. So, I stayed on the floor and looked straight ahead, avoiding eye contact with Samuel, knowing he was in good hands with my mom. My peripheral vision caught glimpses of him. Amid the speeches, clapping and cheers, all I could hear was "Mama, Mama, Mama!"

Next was brunch in the House members' family lounge. The long rectangular room was packed with toddlers running around and families picking over muffins, warm fruit and cold eggs, potatoes and bacon. It was another loud, overstimulating environment, with a plentiful supply of germs. Many of the kids had their first colds of the season.

We met more people whose names we wouldn't remember until we were introduced again later in the session. We visited Rick's new office again, imagining where the family photos, plaques and plants would go. We took in the panoramic views of Tallahassee from the top floor and walked around the rotunda. Then it was over.

It was a preview of the 60 days to come beginning the first Tuesday in March. Some states' legislators work throughout the year. Not Florida. If all went well, the first Friday in May would be *sine die*, the end of session. Sixty days to craft bills, find co-sponsors, work through committee meetings, and then debate on the House floor, isn't much time to make an idea a law.

Within these walls, state representatives meet their new best friends. Lobbyists always want "just five minutes" to make a good impression. They are unelected, but unapologetically political and powerful. It's like another chess game, but with different rules that require new strategies.

Elected officials must strike a balance between wielding power from the political pulpit and understanding the sacred duty political office should command. It didn't take long for me to understand what the late Aneurin Bevan, a prominent British politician, meant when he said, "Politics is blood sport."

I didn't know any of this on swearing-in day. There was no ceremony for me, but my application to become a six-year legislative spouse was approved on election night. In the absence of Cliff's Notes, mentors and confidantes, I learned how to cope at home while Rick lived in Tallahassee for 60 days. A bigger stage brought more access, privilege and opportunity. It was ours to have if we wanted it, but did we deserve it? Common sense and our moral compasses were our guides.

Competition reigned, and partisanship was the weapon of choice. Those in the majority might deny that, but I watched Rick serve in the minority and super-minority as one of the few elected Democrats. During one session, House leadership didn't like how Rick spoke in opposition to oil drilling legislation after the Deepwater Horizon spill. Rick had been the ranking Democrat on the Energy committee for the 2006-2008 and 2008-2010 sessions. After speaking out, he lost his seat on the Energy Committee for the 2010-2012 sessions. When Rick opposed a bill that related to legislators testifying under oath in court cases, he was seemingly punished again. This stemmed from Rick's decision to release documents on the travel industry's failure to pay state sales taxes. Speaker Dean Cannon retaliated by refusing to have Rick's proposed bill that would have outlawed the discriminatory practices some condominium associations employ against guide dog users heard on the floor.

During legislative sessions, Tallahassee can be like a Garden of Eden. Weeknights consist of lobbyist-sponsored dinners, where food, alcohol and opportunity abound. Part of my job as a legislative spouse was to keep Rick grounded. Egos can balloon as big as the bubble in which the politicians reside. The first year, Rick rented an apartment off Apalachee Parkway. A few other representatives lived in the same complex. I congratulated Rick on his election to the Legislature by giving him the boxed set of *The West Wing*.

Instead of hanging out in the bars after business dinners, Rick and Reps. Keith Fitzgerald and Scott Randolph spent most evenings by watching politics play out on DVDs through the lives of *West Wing*'s Jed Bartlet and Toby Ziegler. Politicos who partied would be hung over the next day. Rick preferred to be a legislator who was well-prepared and rested.

After the swearing-in, Rick needed to stay in Tallahassee for a few more days to attend meetings. He kept the car and the luggage and hailed a cab for the kids and me. Our flight home to St. Pete was the first of many goodbyes in this new city.

Kerry, Jordan and Samuel in the Florida Capitol
with guide dog in training, Jim

— Chapter 6 —

BREAK A LEG

With the holidays behind us, 2007 began with more travel to Tallahassee for Rick. Before the annual 60-day session began in March, legislators spent several weeks in committee meetings.

His new job was to help craft legislation that lawmakers would find worthy of becoming law. Some initiatives were bold: increase safety for first responders; protect defenseless children; advocate for the elderly and people with disabilities; preserve our natural resources and environment. It seemed to me that some of the bills proposed by other legislators favored special interest groups. I was a new legislative spouse, but I could already tell that altruism was in short supply. I wondered what, if anything, a newcomer and Democrat like Rick could accomplish in a chamber dominated by Republicans.

I was astounded to learn that some proposed bills were pre-ordained to become law before the session even began. Was the lobbying of colleagues and sincere promotion of Rick's bills in vain?

Rick was living apart from our family on a reduced salary in a job that was more than full time with the hope of improving the lives of his constituents. Those in control often wielded power without ever engaging in meaningful debate.

Survival meant working across the aisle. Rick's only hope for accomplishing anything meaningful in 60 days was to befriend and engage colleagues whose political ideologies were opposite his. His inauguration was also mine. From a distance, I listened as he described life in Tallahassee during the session. We both quickly learned what games were played. It was frustrating to hear how hard it sometimes was to simply have a bill considered in committee.

With then Sen. Barack Obama, discussing the issues in 2007

During Rick's six-year tenure in the Legislature, I logged at least 20 600-mile round trips to Tallahassee with the kids. We honed our routines. Pack the bags, snacks, DVDs and go. The drive became second nature. I memorized the order in which we'd reach each town along the way, learned the cleanest stops for bathroom breaks and knew the last McDonald's where I could get a large $1 coffee.

When we saw the brown-and-white signs that read "Forest Capital Museum State Park," we knew we were in Perry, less than an hour from Tallahassee. Semi-trailer trucks packed high with logs seemed to appear out of nowhere. "Samuel, look at the Lincoln Logs," I'd exclaim as the trucks whizzed by, shaking our van. He was at the height of his car and truck phase, so this leg of the trip amused him.

We sometimes bumped into other legislative families who were in Tallahassee for the weekend, but many lawmakers moved their families there during the session. Some families were surprised when I told them the kids and I remained in St. Pete and commuted on weekends. The arrangement worked for us, and I knew I was luckier than many parents who must go it alone because death, divorce or overseas military service have taken their partners out of the picture.

What I did was nothing extraordinary or special. Spending week-days without Rick was a decision we had made together, and it was temporary. I didn't work outside the home during the first 10 years of Rick's political career, but my days were still packed with childcare, housekeeping, cooking and volunteering – lots of volunteering. I immersed myself in the work of the Junior League. I volunteered at the kids' schools as a parent driver for most field trips. As a class parent, I served as a liaison between the teachers and other parents. I volunteered in the school library. I led an art enrichment committee. I served on local nonprofit boards dedi-cated to improving the lives of children and families.

I confess that I was frustrated and lonely at times. Sometimes I wondered if we had made the right decision. Would it have been easier to take the kids out of school instead of logging thousands of miles commuting back and forth? Jordan was a good student who could independently complete assignments in the back seat of the car. Her private school would've bent over backward to provide les-sons, online assistance and daily phone conferences. She wouldn't have struggled to keep up, but she would miss her friends, ballet classes and Irish step dancing lessons.

I knew that preschool wasn't critical to later academic success, yet I worried about uprooting Samuel, too. Maybe the other wives were right in following their husbands. There was no reason I couldn't teach Samuel social skills and provide enrichment activities. Our dogs were family, and they were big. Henry was a 90-pound black Labrador. Betsy was smaller, but both would not have been accept-ed in a hotel or apartment.

When Rick was in Tallahassee, we followed a schedule to ensure that he stayed at least somewhat involved in the kids' lives. My cell phone rang every weekday morning around 7:30 during the 20-minute drive to Jordan's school. Rick and I said quick hellos before I'd pass the phone to Jordan in the back seat. She'd give Rick a rundown of the day, what was happening in school, what she watched on television the night before or what she'd be practicing at dance that afternoon. Then, she'd pass the phone to Samuel. Rick would manage to extract a few words out of him before he gave the phone back to Jordan, who passed it back to me. Rick briefed me on the day's agenda: his schedule, who he'd be meeting with, what committee meetings were on the calendar and which fundraiser or industry dinner he'd attend that evening.

I relished the predictability of these conversations, but they were often peppered with "Hey, how are you? See you soon. Great to see you." There was always someone in the background who wanted to say hello to Rick. He had the phone to his ear, but if someone wanted to speak to him, they interrupted. It didn't matter that it was his wife or one of his kids on the other end.

Eventually, I accepted the interruptions as part of my new reality. Entering an elevator signaled the end of our conversation.

"I might lose you," Rick would say. That would be the last time I'd hear from him until dinner time, save for occasional texts throughout the day.

Evening events were part of a legislator's life. I knew not to expect Rick's dinnertime call the night of the annual softball game between the Democrat and Republican legislators. That morning, he told me he'd call around 8 p.m. When I didn't hear from him by 8:30, I called him so he could say goodnight to the kids. His conversation with them was brief. He told me he'd call me later. I figured the game wasn't over.

About an hour later, Rick did call - from the emergency room of Capital Regional Hospital. He had tried to leg out a ground ball to the Republican shortstop, but he tripped over first base and landed awkwardly on the unforgiving clay.

He was likely still in shock from the pain because he chuckled as he recounted that even though the game was sponsored by the state firefighters and paramedics union, none of the union members in the stands came over to assist as he lay writhing in pain. Rick's right tibia was fractured. He declined surgery and was on his way home with a fistful of prescriptions for pain and a cast from his upper thigh to his ankle.

Rick will be the first to admit he inherited his father's stubbornness. I don't see it often, but that night he insisted he didn't need me. I knew better.

I told him I'd be there the next day. He told me his legislative aide, Kevin King, and another House member, Keith Fitzgerald, would take care of him, but Rick didn't realize how much help he would need in the coming weeks.

He was only halfway through his first legislative session and still negotiating a new political landscape. Soon, he'd have to navigate the narrow Capitol halls in a wheelchair.

It was only Tuesday. I emailed the kids' teachers to tell them they'd be absent the rest of the week. I arranged for our regular sitter to feed and walk the dogs twice a day for the next five days. I packed three suitcases.

Seeing Rick in that much pain was hard. He'd sustained a torn ACL on a ski trip 10 years earlier, but this was different. He was stoic, though. He also found it funny that he was living one of his favorite Jimmy Buffett songs. The words from "Growing Older but Not Up," could've been written about Rick: *I rounded first, never thought of the worst, as I studied the shortstop's position. Crack went my leg like the shell of an egg. Someone call a decent physician.*

Rick watched movies with the kids while I rented a shower seat, filled prescriptions, did laundry and stocked his fridge. We could only stay until Sunday, and I feared leaving him alone and in pain. I made sure he was able to get himself out of bed and pull his pants over the bulky caSt. Kevin and Keith promised to drive him to the Capitol every day. Rick was able to make coffee and cereal for himself each morning. Lunch was always at the Capitol Members' Dining Room and he never missed the evening events, which almost always included dinner.

Rick believed he could drive, but there was no way he could fit into the driver's seat. The cast prevented him from bending his leg to control the pedals. It would be that way for six weeks. Instead of letting his car sit at the apartment complex for the next four weeks, I enlisted a family friend to drive it home to St. Pete. The kids and I spent each remaining weekend of the session in Tallahassee.

We went on outings that could entertain the kids and were accessible to wheelchair users. Pushing Rick in and out of doorways, onto elevators and through restaurants opened my eyes to what life is like for people who must live this way every day. Sometimes, people cut in front of us on the way to an elevator or doorway. They could run. I was pushing my husband with two children in tow.

Rick discovered how poorly designed the Capitol building is for people with disabilities. Finding your way as a freshman lawmaker is a challenge. Wheeling yourself through narrow hallways with many turns while balancing a briefcase on your lap took finesse. The first Friday of May marks the end of the legislative session in Florida. I got there the day before to pack up the apartment and bring Rick home.

We had thought it would be good idea for him to rent an apartment, so there would be plenty of room when the kids and I came to visit. That meant renting furniture for two bedrooms and the living room. We bought a television, sheets, comforters, towels and kitchen tools. We'd been naïve to think that Rick would use the kitchen as if it were our home in St. Pete. When it was time to return to St. Pete, Rick was still using a wheelchair and unable to stand longer than a few minutes at a time. I packed the entire apartment and loaded everything including the television into the car. The only remaining space was for us.

Rick was happy to see Jordan, Samuel and my mom waiting for him when we pulled up to the house. A few weeks later, the cast came off and the crutches became his constant companions for the next six months. It was a challenging time, but we managed to take our planned vacation to Boston and Bar Harbor, Maine, that summer. Recovering from a broken leg was never going to hold Rick back. On crutches, he chased down a Boston subway operator who closed the doors too quickly, leaving 9-year-old Jordan standing alone at the stop behind us. Rick even climbed a couple hundred feet on crutches to pose for a family picture atop Cadillac Mountain in Acadia National Park. By October, he was off crutches and ready to head back to Tallahassee for committee meetings.

In the next session, Rick would have the benefit of being seasoned and uninjured. We were prepared. Contemplating our upcoming separations was easier this time. I knew what to expect. I was an expert at keeping things running smoothly at home without Rick. I was a three-time campaign alum, experienced legislative spouse, and juggler of everything else.

That first year Rick served in Tallahassee we learned to lean on each other in ways we hadn't before. He needed me to take care of him. I needed him to remind me sometimes that even though we were apart, we were committed to each other. Our family unit was strong.

Rick's second year in Tallahassee would be marked by new challenges that would make a broken leg and separation seem inconsequential.

Chapter 7

WHEN THE SMOKE CLEARS

It was 3 a.m. when the phone rang in our hotel room in Colonial Williamsburg, Virginia, where we were vacationing and indulging our daughter's new-found interest in American history.

"Your home is on fire," my dad told me. "It's a total loss."

My whole body shook. After I hung up, I got in the shower and stood under the cold water until I stopped shaking. Rick was reading breaking news on his laptop. There were already pictures of our burning home on the internet.

We needed to get back to St. Pete and what was left of our home. We packed, then woke Jordan and Samuel. By 5 a.m., we were at a Starbucks getting coffee and scones. For the next 14 hours, we took turns charging our cell phones in the only outlet in my Acura MDX while we fielded calls from our insurance company, family, friends and reporters.

News of the fire circulated among Rick's House colleagues, who he'd said goodbye to just three weeks earlier when session ended. Members from both sides of the aisle offered support and condolences. Gov. Charlie Crist, who is from St. Pete, offered help and prayers.

I put my hand over my left ear while Rick took calls so I could hear Jeff Ulevich, the firefighter who had rescued our Labradors, Henry and Maggie. He told me that he had given Henry oxygen and that it was a good sign that Maggie wanted to drink water.

For hours, I repeated answers to the same questions my family and friends asked. We were okay. We were lucky. We didn't know how it happened.

We didn't know yet if there was anything we needed. We didn't know how much was lost.

My mom texted photos of Henry and Maggie from the emergency veterinarian's office. That was the first time we smiled that morning. It didn't matter what was lost if Henry and Maggie were okay.

About an hour before we got to St. Pete, Rick's legislative aide, Kevin King, called. Reporters wanted to know what time we would be home. They told Kevin they wanted to film us walking through our home for the first time after the fire. No way, we said. Rick was a state representative, but that gave no one the right to witness our emotions when we saw our burned home for the first time.

Kevin enlisted the help of two St. Petersburg police officers to secure all entry points to our house. An officer even stayed in his cruiser in case the media showed up. I was grateful to them for protecting our privacy.

Earlier that day, a friend whose sister survived a house fire warned us that Jordan and Samuel should not see their burned home. The psychological impact of seeing their destroyed belongings could be worse than the material losses. We already had decided they would never see the house, even when Samuel later asked if we could drive by. Jordan and Samuel were 10 and 5, which made it easier for Rick and me to keep them from seeing news stories and photos of the fire.

Before we went to the house, we met our sitter at Panera so she could get dinner for Jordan and Samuel. Then, we met Mom, Kevin and the police officer at our home.

It was dusk, so we took a cursory tour of the remains before heading to Athenian Garden to eat before getting the kids. We picked at our food, not knowing what to say to each other. We hadn't thought of where we would sleep that night, but a family friend offered to let us stay in the condo she kept for out-of-town guests.

Every day for the next week, we dropped the kids off with friends, then drove to the house to cull through what was left of our belongings. The fire inspector determined that the fire began in an outside electrical outlet in the front of our home. Once sparked, the fire traveled up to the attic and festered for a while before the master bedroom, bathroom and closet ceilings imploded. Had we been home and somehow slept through the smoke, the ceiling would've fallen on Rick and me.

The kids' rooms were on the other side of the house. They were a mess, but their toys, clothes and stuffed animals sustained only smoke and water damage. Saving some of their favorite things was a small consolation when the veterinarian called the next day to tell us that Henry, our beloved companion for six years, had died. We had planned to visit him the next morning. Now, we didn't even have a chance to say goodbye.

Our vet converted his extra bathroom into a hospital room for Maggie. Soft music played while she rested, hooked up to an I.V., on a doggie bed. She wagged her tail every time we visited over the next three days, until the vet called with more bad news. The smoke damage to her lungs was irreversible. We'd adopted her from Labrador Retriever Rescue of Florida three months earlier. We were still just getting to know her when she succumbed to the irreversible smoke damage to her lungs and the burns on her body. We were devastated but continued the machinations of saving what personal possessions were salvageable, looking for rental homes, negotiating our homeowner's insurance claim and seeking a contractor to build a new home on the same lot where our burned one sat.

June marks the start of rainy season in Florida. Since our home no longer had a roof, we worked quickly to save what we could. I was glad that there were a few photo albums that hadn't made it into the attic, where everything was destroyed. We still had some family photos even if our wedding album was gone. We'd been married 14 years, but I hadn't had my wedding dress preserved. It hung in the protective bag in the section of my closet that hadn't burned. Maybe Jordan would be able to wear it someday.

We decided to build a new home on the same lot. After meeting with three contractors, we hired the brothers who grew up next door and used to mow our lawn. We were in a hurry to return to normal, and they promised to work as fast as possible.

In the first six months of 2008, we had lost Rick's mom to Alzheimer's disease, my Aunt Amy to cancer and our dogs to the fire. Losing our home meant that for the first time in our lives we were on the receiving end of others' generosity. We had homeowner's insurance, but the settlement money didn't cover all our losses. Friends donated gift cards so we could buy necessities like toilet paper, cleaning supplies and towels for our rental home. Temple Beth-El, where we are members, organized a meal train that lasted for two months. Our friends from Samuel's preschool hosted a toy party for the kids.

While Jordan and Samuel were at day camp, I combed through our financial records that survived the blaze for receipts from furniture purchases. We had to prove to our insurance company how much it would cost to buy what was lost at today's prices.

I was working in a conference room at Rick's legislative office when Junior League President Jenn Maxwell walked in. She gave me an envelope full of checks from league members who wanted to help our family. A few weeks earlier, the league had given me an award for my service. Now the same women who nominated me for the award were helping our family through this tragedy.

We were not alone.

Still, I felt guilty. I thought of those who experienced fires but unlike us had no insurance, family or friends close by. We were lucky. Our family was intact. The car that would've been parked in the garage the night of the fire was unharmed. We had our cell phones, wedding rings, a week's worth of clothes and each other.

A few weeks later, the weekend before my 40th birthday, we went to Orlando for a legislative conference. We were still reeling from the fire, but we were eager for a weekend away.

On our first day in Orlando, Rick attended meetings, then headed to the golf course with colleagues. Jordan, Samuel and I were enjoying "Muppet Vision 3D" at Hollywood Studios when my phone rang.

"You need to come back to the hotel," Rick said.

"But we're in the middle of a show," I said.

"The doctor's office called. You need to come now," he said.

I walked fast toward the Goofy parking lot, pulling Samuel by the hand while Jordan ran to keep up. I picked Rick up and drove to Florida Hospital in Celebration, just as his doctor had instructed.

Our brief respite was over. A battle of a different kind was beginning.

— Chapter 8 —

A TIME TO HEAL

The bruises on Rick's arms and hips and the tiny red dots around his ankles had been there for several weeks. He blamed the large one on his hip from his cell phone case pressing against his skin. Someone would've had to hit him to leave the red and purple marks.

Rick and I never said a word to each other about them. For the last month, our conversations had revolved around grieving, cleaning and planning. We saw the bruises, but we didn't realize they signified a life-threatening condition.

Rick had just finished playing golf with legislative colleagues and lobbyists when he listened to a voice message from his primary care doctor in St. Pete, who said his bloodwork revealed a dangerously low platelet count. A normal platelet count ranges from 150 to 450 platelets per liter of blood. Rick had 5. He needed to go to the hospital. Rick asked if he could wait until we got back to St. Pete. His doctor said no. If he were in an accident or hit his head, he could bleed to death.

I picked Rick up at the hotel, and we drove to Florida Hospital. The doctor gave Rick the choice to check in to the hospital for treatment, or head home to follow up with his physician. Armed with steroids to boost his platelet count and a missive to see his doctor Monday morning, we decided to head back to St. Pete. The doctor at Florida Hospital left me with strict instructions for Rick not to drive, ride a bicycle, or do anything strenuous. We were both scared. We decided to go to the emergency room at St. Anthony's Hospital the next day.

Jordan and Samuel stayed with Mom while I went with Rick to the E.R. A CT scan ruled out bleeding on his brain. By now, his platelet count was 2. By dinnertime, he was admitted to a room. I picked up the kids, got takeout and joined Rick in his hospital room for dinner. He had already had one dose of a high level of dexamethasone. Steroids temporarily increased his platelet count, but the tradeoff was insomnia and headaches.

It was the night before my 40th birthday, but that was the last thing on my mind. We were living in a rental house while trying to rebuild our lives. My husband was in the hospital while doctors tried to figure out why his platelets were so dangerously low. They tested him for cancer, leukemia and blood disorders. Thankfully, all those tests came back negative. But we still had no answers.

By the next day, Rick's platelet count was high enough for the hospital to release him. He continued taking steroids and having his blood counts checked every week. The steroids were hard on his body, so the doctors tried to decrease the level. When they did, his platelet count fell. It was a cycle of pills, blood tests, waiting and more pills.

A family friend who is an oncologist suggested Rick might have ITP, idiopathic thrombocytopenia purpura. Idiopathic means "of unknown origin." Thrombocytopenia is a condition characterized by abnormally low levels of platelets. Children diagnosed with ITP usually outgrow the disorder. Supposedly this was incurable in adults. Steroids raised Rick's platelets, but we knew that wasn't a long-term solution because of the impact on his organs. Doctors finally confirmed that Rick had ITP. The next task was to determine how to control it so he could live without the fear of bleeding to death.

Amid all the losses that year, and now Rick's illness, he finally caught a break. No one qualified to oppose him for reelection. He could focus on getting well without having to campaign. The extra time we had because he wasn't running a campaign meant that we could focus on his health, the well-being of Jordan and Samuel, and select furniture, paint colors, kitchen and bathroom cabinets, and all the accessories we needed for our new home.

Another bright spot was our new rescue dog, Peppermint, a black Labrador. Our landlord was kind enough to allow us to adopt her while still living in the rental home. Peppermint, who was given up because she supposedly didn't get along with other dogs, rescued us from our sadness and was an affable companion to the nine puppies that we would raise for Southeastern Guide Dogs over the next nine years.

Construction of our new home progressed steadily. Life was inching toward a new normal, yet Rick's ITP remained uncured. If it took him longer than 20 minutes to call me with the results after a blood test, I panicked. I assumed that when he did call, he would tell me he had cancer. I had become conditioned to expect bad news.

When Rick returned to Tallahassee for the 2009 session, he planned his commutes to accommodate Rituxan infusions, a new course of therapy that allowed him to get off the steroids. The medicine is used to treat some types of cancer, such as non-Hodgkin's lymphoma and chronic lymphocytic leukemia. He would spend several hours sitting among chemotherapy patients while the medicine flowed through his veins. It wasn't a cure, but it was better than living with the side effects of steroids.

That spring, people in political circles encouraged Rick to run for mayor of St. Petersburg. It was rumored that two former council colleagues, Bill Foster and Kathleen Ford, were going to run. In politics, timing really is everything. Deciding to run and when to announce your candidacy, launch an ad or roll out endorsements are strategically scheduled. A candidate's actions are predicated on getting the best media coverage, which can elevate the campaign.

"It's Time," the slogan for Rick's first legislative campaign in 2006, meant that it was time for a new representative for District 53. His first state House campaign ad was called "Rick Time." Every time Rick ran for office, the decision was ours. He always said he couldn't and wouldn't run without my blessing. With four campaigns behind us, and 10 years of our lives invested in politics, a decision for higher office required many conversations together and with our consultants. We decided that 2009 was not the year for Rick to run for mayor.

It would have been Rick's biggest political job yet. People thought he'd make a good mayor, which was flattering. Many assumed it was a logical next step. Leading Florida's fifth largest city was always in the back of his mind, but his health needed to be fully restored.

The day before the 2009 legislative session ended, I received the keys to our new home. Instead of celebrating the end of session with other lawmakers, Rick came home that night. He hadn't been home for most of the month, so he had only seen the photos that I texted to him.

The 2,700-square-foot home was built in less than a year. Our builders had kept their promise to do what they could to help us return to normal. But even a beautiful home with brand new everything can't erase the stress and worry that comes with a significant health issue.

Until we had a solution for Rick's ITP, we couldn't move forward. We eventually found a doctor who suggested that Rick's platelets could be getting trapped in his spleen. A small organ that many of us take for granted, the spleen performs the task of filtering blood as part of the immune system. Old red blood cells are recycled in the spleen, and platelets and white blood cells are stored there. The doctor suspected that Rick's spleen saw the platelets as foreign and destroyed them.

A splenectomy that October was successful in curing Rick's ITP. He returned to Tallahassee for the 2010 session and won reelection later that year to a third term, but life as a legislator was wearing on him. The political landscape in Tallahassee made it difficult for a Democrat to pass legislation in a sea of Republicans. Partisanship was increasingly pervasive in such a toxic environment. It was hard to find common ground with adversaries. Term limits meant that Rick could run once more in 2012 for another two-year term, but he instead decided to return to the practice of law full time while he focused on trying to answer the question many were asking him.

On a Sunday in late fall 2012, Rick and I invited two of his advisors to our home for a discussion. The four of us sat around the table on our back patio while we discussed a possible run for mayor of St. Petersburg.

"Don't start training a new dog during the campaign..." were the first words out of his longtime advisor's mouth. I knew what he was referring to. We had raised three guide dog puppies for Southeastern Guide Dogs. Puppies can be like babies. Sometimes they're loud. Sometimes they have accidents in public. Sometimes they get all the attention. Our advisor, who was also a friend, had Rick's best interests at heart. Should Rick run for mayor, he didn't want anything to detract from what Rick needed to do, which was win.

I understood what he meant, but I was annoyed that someone was in our home telling us we should not continue volunteering for a cause we were committed to because of an election.

I knew that if Rick were to run for mayor, it would be the biggest race of his political career. Our lives would change again. More disruption to our family life, increased scrutiny of him as a candidate and person, and how he would reintroduce himself to the voters of St. Petersburg and differentiate himself from the incumbent were just a few of the topics we discussed.

This time, however, our kids were older, I was working, and we both had the benefit of being campaign veterans. This was the right time.

I told him, "If you're going to run, then you need to win."

— Chapter 9 —

DEMOCRATS DON'T
WEAR RED

Rick and I walked hand in hand down the steps of City Hall, smiling as the media snapped photographs. It was Feb. 11, 2013, the day Rick filed to run for St. Petersburg mayor. As we descended the steps with Jordan and Samuel, it felt like I was jumping headfirst off the high dive into an unfamiliar pool.

In each previous political race, Rick quietly filed the campaign paperwork and started campaigning. When you're applying to be the CEO of your city, it's news. His quest to be mayor also meant that he would be campaigning against his former City Council colleague, incumbent Mayor Bill Foster.

Rick entered the race as a former state legislator who hadn't been on the ballot in three years. He had to reintroduce himself as a candidate, craft his platform and convince St. Pete voters that he was not only an alternative to the incumbent but the best choice to move the city forward. Joining him on the ballot were three-time mayoral candidate Kathleen Ford, also a former council colleague, and political newcomers Anthony Cates and Paul Congemi.

Mayor Foster had done a respectable job leading the city through the Great Recession. However, after three years, several key issues remained unresolved: Among them were the future of The Pier, the iconic inverted pyramid that was structurally unsound, and whether the owners of the Tampa Bay Rays would keep the team in St. Pete.

The "no dog training" comment from Rick's longtime political advisor several weeks earlier caught me off guard, but I knew that everyone supporting Rick wanted to leave nothing to chance. Our plans to raise another puppy for Southeastern Guide Dogs could wait until the campaign was over. Rick had just over six months until the August primary.

My job as a political spouse was to support from the sidelines and help when asked. Rick's first job was to hire a campaign manager. Political candidates in St. Petersburg rarely used full-time political consultants, even after 1993, when voters approved a city charter amendment creating a strong-mayor system. Some candidates' races were run by friends who volunteered their time but had no political experience. But Rick believed in hiring professionals with strong political backgrounds who would best position him to win.

Rick and I selected a 24-year-old political operative from South Florida whose most recent job was running a state Senate campaign where his boss won by 17 votes. Cesar Fernandez was young enough to be our son, but he had the political chops of a seasoned professional. Often on the campaign trail, voters mistook Cesar for Rick's son, even while our own 10-year-old son was standing by his side.

Cesar and four other 20-somethings ran a well-oiled campaign for Rick. The team used social media to tell Rick's story, a new way to reach voters that cost less than television and radio ads. This was before paid political ads on social media became the norm. All of them unmarried and without children, the campaign team devoted most of their time to the campaign, often working more than 70 hours a week. I'd walk into the war room, as they called it, and no one looked up. They weren't rude. They were hyper-focused on analyzing data, developing call lists, creating canvassing maps and researching fundraising prospects.

As momentum for Rick's campaign grew, so did the questions. People asked me why he would be the best choice to lead our city.

The campaign message and tenets "listen, learn and lead" became my 30-second elevator speech. Visitors to Creative Clay, where I was the public relations manager, sometimes popped their heads into my office when they saw my nameplate to ask my opinion on an issue. Those moments were my chance to hook the audience and gain support for Rick. But I was careful to do it quietly. I was certain that my colleagues supported Rick, but even in a casual work environment, campaigning is not appropriate. Further, my employer annually applied for grants from the City of St. Petersburg for arts funding. Part of my job was to write grants. A year earlier, I'd reached out to Mayor Foster to apply for a donation of a used city van to transport our artists. Rick hadn't won yet, but I realized that even as the spouse of a mayoral candidate, I would have to maintain a neutral position in the workplace. At my request, I stopped working on any portion of my employer's grants for the City of St. Petersburg. My role in lobbying the city for funding could be viewed as a conflict of interest, and I believed it was. I didn't want anything to distract from the campaign, should any candidate or the public decide to make it an issue.

It also wasn't uncommon for parents and teachers at the kids' schools to approach me in the car line to ask about Rick's stance on an issue.

"Tell me your husband's top three priorities should he be elected mayor," was the most often asked question. After six campaigns, I knew it was essential to not just repeat campaign talking points, but to understand what his priorities as mayor would be and how they would impact St. Pete residents.

No one trained me on the talking points. I listened while Rick talked to his campaign team on the phone in our home office while I worked on the other computer. I learned what his plan was to resolve the stalemate with the Rays and how he would craft a committee to review designs, with public input, for a new Pier. Those weren't the only issues I would tell voters about when asked. I told anyone who inquired that Rick would advocate for small businesses, affordable housing, and racial equity.

A week in a campaign can seem like an eternity, yet everything seems urgent. Campaigns are a Red Bull-free source of adrenaline. Keeping your eye on the ball is key. We never considered how winning would look or feel. Distractions from the goal are like curve balls that send the batter back to the dugout after a strikeout. We celebrated small victories that moved the needle, such as endorsements, positive polling or a good fundraising period.

It had been seven years since we filmed our first political commercial. In June, John Rowley came back to St. Pete to film the first commercial for Rick's mayoral campaign. I was given an address and told that the kids and I were to report to a home in the Woodlawn neighborhood at 2 p.m. on filming day. Around 8 the night before the shoot, Rick called to tell me he was headed home – with John.

When Rick and John walked through the front door, they headed straight to our walk-in closet. I followed, pulling Peppermint and Sarah, the Southeastern Guide Dog puppy in training we were watching (not raising!), off John.

"Don't worry," he said. "I have dogs, too." Still, I was embarrassed. Our dogs were jumping all over him while he pulled dress shirts and ties off the racks, putting together Rick's wardrobe for the next day.

John told me to make sure Rick did not wear a red tie. Democrats don't wear red in political ads, even though this was a nonpartisan election.

I waited to see if he had an opinion on what the kids and I should wear.

The 2013 Closet Tour lasted all of five minutes. John was practically out the front door when he said, "Bring the dog." He meant Sarah, the 1-year-old black Labrador in training.

The campaign had begun with the edict, "No Dogs." Now, a dog that wasn't ours was cast in the first commercial of Rick's mayoral campaign.

I called to John: "What should I wear?'

"Wear something bright," he said. "No patterns, stripes or plaids." I combed my closet and found some fuchsia pants. I broke the "no stripes" rule and paired them with a colorful, billowy, belted top. Jordan's knee-length sky blue dress complimented Samuel's khaki pants and white oxford shirt that was absent of the Ralph Lauren polo horse, and Sperry topsiders.

We reprised our 2006 roles of mom and kids on an afternoon walk, but this time with an adorable and well-behaved black Labrador. The kids walked confidently without me holding their tiny hands. I held Sarah's pink leash in my left hand as she proudly walked with her head up and chest out, as if she were our family pet. When the ads started running on television, we called Sarah our good luck charm.

Rick's campaign continued an upward trajectory, but we took nothing for granted when endorsements and contributions rolled in. That meant no family vacation that summer. Weekends were dedicated to canvassing neighborhoods to reach as many voters as possible. The only time the kids and I traveled was in late July to deliver Jordan to a weeklong summer program at Georgetown University. Samuel and I spent the week in Washington, D.C., and took the Amtrak to visit my aunt in New Jersey. The team felt the campaign was in good shape, so they let Rick fly to Washington on his birthday before we picked up Jordan the next day.

This election was the first time Rick had a primary. Shortly after polls closed on Aug. 24, we arrived at The Palladium Theatre. We could hear the music downstairs in the room that hosted jazz concerts. The last time I was in that room was in 2007, when Jordan danced in *The Nutcracker*. It housed the costumes, kids, props and parent volunteers.

Primary night 2013, Rick and Jordan and Kerry
with campaign manager Cesar Fernandez. Photo credit: Michael Flanagan

We were hopeful, but we didn't know the results until Cesar came backstage with the news. Rick received the second highest number of votes in the primary. He and Mayor Foster would be in a runoff on Nov. 8.

A few days before the general election, Cesar told Rick he wanted to book the presidential suite at The Vinoy, St. Pete's ritziest hotel. Rick had done everything he could to position himself to win, but I couldn't let myself imagine a win that would warrant a night of celebrating in the presidential suite.

We were hopeful, but we prepared ourselves to wake up the next morning, head to our respective jobs and resume life as before. No matter the outcome, I was proud of the honorable and respectable campaign Rick ran.

Election day began with a 7 a.m. trip to the polls. We took the kids with us before they went to school. The media wanted to capture us walking in as a family to vote. They did the same with the Foster family. Reporters wanted to know Rick's feelings about the election, his final message to voters and predictions for voter turnout.

Later that morning, I joined Rick at Kopper Kitchen, a popular breakfast spot in our neighborhood. Between bites of scrambled eggs and toast, many voters told Rick they'd already voted for him. It was good news, but election day is the longest day of a campaign. The polls wouldn't close for several more hours.

Rick spent the rest of the day visiting polling sites, talking to voters, and giving interviews. I cleaned the house. The few hours I had to perform rote activities before I picked up Samuel at school was a salve for my nerves.

Later that afternoon, I packed our overnight bags for the Vinoy. I still didn't know why the campaign had booked two rooms for our family and the presidential suite. It would be a night of celebration, or a thank you party for staffers and volunteers. If Rick didn't win, I would have preferred to come home and sleep in our own beds.

We checked in at The Vinoy around 5 p.m. We ordered room service, showered, then dressed. Rick and Samuel wore suits. Jordan and I wore dresses. I was too superstitious to make a big deal out of buying a new dress for election night. Hours before, I found a brown A-line dress at TJ Maxx with a lace overlay. I hadn't even tried it on, but it fit perfectly and would be comfortable during what I suspected would be a long night.

Cesar told us to arrive at NOVA 535 at 8 p.m. On the 10-minute ride from The Vinoy to NOVA, Rick made small talk with the Uber driver while I asked myself a long list of questions that no one could answer.

Would it be a late night, or would everyone be gone by 9?

Did we make it to every last neighborhood where there were many undecided voters?

Did I tell my family where the party was?

Did we feed the dogs before we left the house?

Did I put the alarm on?

Did I tell all our friends about the party?

What did the latest poll say?

Do we have our hotel keys?

Will the kids be okay in a hotel room by themselves?

Why can't we just go home after the party?

I kept these questions to myself.

Soon enough, I would have an answer to the only remaining question: Who would be the next mayor of St. Petersburg?

— Chapter 10 —

NEW TITLES

We exited the sedan in a dark alley behind NOVA 535. "Celebration" by Kool & the Gang blared. The crowd roared. It sounded like a Saturday night, but it was Tuesday. Election night. Jordan and I walked gingerly toward the back entrance, careful not to get our heels stuck in the spaces between the uneven red bricks.

Cesar was hurrying us inside, but I told the kids to stop, stand together and pose for a photo. We didn't know there were media trucks lining the space in front of the building on busy MLK Street North. Reporters were waiting to go live with election results. I wanted to remember the smiles on the kids' faces, their arms linked, proud of their dad. The kids had grown up in politics; it was a big night for them, too. When I see that photo of Jordan towering over Samuel in my Facebook memories every year, I'm glad I had the presence of mind to capture that moment.

Candidates don't just walk into their own party and work the crowd. From beginning to end, the evening is choreographed by the campaign team. On the way upstairs, I caught a glimpse of the packed room. It looked like a nightclub. People were enjoying themselves. Some were dancing. Candidates and their families are the last to enjoy campaign night festivities, but what I saw on the way to the holding room full of mirrors, plush velvet-covered furniture and makeup lights was promising.

Campaigns rely on data to determine strategy, pinpoint weak areas, and formulate effective field operations. A good data team knows exactly where the candidate stands – how many points they're up or down and in which voting precincts they're leading or behind.

Throughout the nine-month campaign, the data had been accurate, one of the reasons Rick was able to steadily climb from third place. Cesar had kept Rick abreast of campaign developments, endorsements and items that needed attention or approval. Leading up to election day, the team analyzed mail-in and early voting data. All signs pointed to an eventual victory, but Cesar didn't want Rick to let up on the gas. A few days before election day, the team determined that it was statistically impossible for Mayor Foster to win reelection. Rick's diligent campaigning until the end secured an 11-point victory.

Rick was a veteran candidate, and I was a seasoned political spouse. Yet, we still didn't have the gut feeling you have when you're certain of an outcome. The mood in the holding room was celebratory. Supporters who made their way past the unofficial bouncer were congratulating Rick. Still, we didn't believe he'd won.

Samuel checking election night returns at NOVA 535 - 2013
Photo credit: Michael Flanagan

Samuel, who had spent many Saturdays canvassing with Rick while I drove Jordan round trip to Tampa for dance classes, sat with the campaign team watching results come in on the supervisor of elections' website. My phone lit up with texts from friends who were waiting downstairs. They wanted to know when we would join the party. Family in Kentucky, California, Georgia and New Jersey texted me. We hadn't looked at social media. We were the last to learn that the campaign was over.

Rick had won!

After a quick champagne toast with the team, Rick, Jordan, Samuel and I held hands and walked single file down the dark stairs through the crowd, to the front of the room. Campaign volunteers hugged and high-fived us as we made our way through the crowd. Some in the crowd rushed the stage. They were excited and wanted to be part of the celebration. I hadn't been in front of a crowd that big since our wedding.

Election Night - 2013

It now made sense to me why Cesar had wanted to book the presidential suite at the Vinoy. The hotel had been the site of many celebrations throughout its history. It hosted famous guests, such as James Stewart, Herbert Hoover, Calvin Coolidge and Babe Ruth. It also served as a military training facility during World War II. After a decades-long closure, it reopened in 1992, the year Rick and I were married.

The Vinoy is where the locals go to sip cocktails while sitting in rocking chairs on the spacious veranda overlooking the calm waters of the Vinoy Basin. When people want to know the nicest place to stay in St. Pete, I tell them to book a room at The Vinoy. It's a popular site for fundraisers, galas and weddings. That night, it was where we celebrated a new beginning and an underdog candidate who moved from third to first in a victory many had said was impossible.

We left NOVA 535 around 10 p.m. to return to The Vinoy. I got the kids settled in their room, then we joined friends, campaign staffers and family members in the presidential suite to celebrate the victory.

The next morning, after only three hours of sleep, Rick showered and dressed in a fresh suit and began a daylong schedule of interviews. I took Jordan to school, then Samuel and I went home to feed Peppermint and a new guide dog in training, Petey, who had come to live with us in August for a few months before going to his trainer.

After dropping Samuel off at school. I walked into work with my wet hair pulled into a ponytail and extra under-eye concealer. My coworkers had decorated my office and left flowers and a big handmade card that said, "Congratulations, First Lady!"

It hadn't hit me yet that Rick's election to mayor meant that I had a title: first lady of St. Petersburg. I was still looking through texts from the night before. Many congratulated me as the new first lady of St. Pete. I'd lived in St. Pete my entire life, save for one year of college in Pittsburgh. I'd never heard the mayor's wife referred to as a first lady. The few dozen texts I received told me otherwise.

After the media coverage the night before and already that day, I knew our family would hold a bigger space in the public eye. I hadn't thought about how it might specifically affect me. I knew from Rick's council days that the spouse of the St. Petersburg mayor doesn't necessarily have a platform, as the spouse of the president or governor might. I knew that I was sometimes held to a higher standard because I was married to a politician, but I didn't know what that meant for me.

Every time someone called me "first lady," I chuckled. I appreciated the acknowledgement that I was a partner to Rick, who was the city's elected leader, but it was a role I never envisioned. Not in high school when my classmate Tricia Ulrich's dad, Bob Ulrich, was mayor. Not when Rick and I said yes to that first City Council run. Not even when he filed to run for mayor. We only focused on getting to election day, not what the days after would look like.

First lady is a title usually reserved for people whose pedigree affords them a natural ascent to the position. That wasn't me. My parents weren't St. Pete natives. After my parents divorced, there were times my mom worked two jobs to support my brother and me. I attended community college and the local university while I lived at home and worked two jobs. If you had asked my friends, no one would've predicted that I would be married to a mayor someday.

It didn't matter whether I sought or pursued the role. But like or not, Rick's new title meant that I also had a new title: first lady. Already, our lives were changing. He was the first mayor-elect in St. Pete to form a transition team. His job unofficially began weeks before he was sworn in. When we went out to eat, other patrons requested selfies with the new mayor. Sometimes, they wanted our whole family to pose.

We hadn't prepared for what life looked like after a win. I realized a win would impact me and my family, but I didn't yet know much would change.

When friends ask how I feel about having a spouse who is a politician, I tell them that all endeavors have positive and negative moments. I always felt that one of the benefits of being in politics was that we knew exactly how people felt about us. Those who didn't like Rick's politics, or his decisions, generally weren't very affable to me or the kids.

One unsolicited comment shortly after Rick became mayor almost left me speechless. It was a suggestion for how Rick could be an effective mayor. Wide-eyed and ready to receive a valuable nugget of advice I could pass on to Rick, I listened as this constituent told me he'd be a great mayor "if he could just stop being so partisan." I'm rarely equipped with a quick comeback, but that day the words flowed. I defended Rick's record of working across the aisle with Republicans when he was in the State house. I finished my response by pointing out that several Republicans donated to Rick's mayoral campaign.

I've learned to recognize "fast friends," people I've never met who pursue me for lunch and conversation. The few times I accepted, I noticed how the conversation was a fact-finding exercise that often revolved around my husband. I learned to be guarded and protective of my time. I learned to distinguish between the people who wanted to spend time with me or with the mayor's wife and whether they viewed me as access to Rick. That is one of the most important lessons any new first lady should learn.

— Chapter 11 —
LESSONS
FOR THE NEW GIRL

A three-day stay in Charleston, South Carolina, was the perfect respite from the post-election events and holiday flurry. Low Country food and historic walking tours on cobblestone streets helped us clear our heads. We returned to St. Pete refreshed and ready for this new chapter in our lives.

The day after we returned was New Year's Eve. Rick would be sworn in as mayor in two days, and I still didn't know what to wear. The night Rick was declared the winner, some people began calling me the first lady. Rick had been groomed for this moment. He was ready to lead the city, but I wasn't sure what my role was supposed to be.

I'd advocated for adoption of foster children, raised puppies to become guide dogs and worked to promote arts equity for people with disabilities. I wondered if I should have a platform, or if that might conflict with Rick's agenda. I didn't want to seem pushy or seek the limelight, yet this new title had me wondering what I was supposed to do.

Rick's new office at City Hall was the first stop the morning of the swearing in. Diplomas, framed award certificates and family photos sat in boxes scattered around the office. The alligator head that had traveled from law offices to legislative offices was already on Rick's new desk. It was a nod to the University of Florida, Rick's alma mater, and a conversation starter for visitors. Less than two months before, Rick was an underdog candidate. In less than an hour, he would be the city's new leader.

The seven weeks from election day to swearing-in day were a blur. We'd met with Junior League members to plan the Mayoral Ball, a *Wizard of Oz*-themed event titled "There's No Place Like St. Petersburg." The event used Rick's election to mayor to raise money for community projects and mentoring and scholarship programs. Between the Thanksgiving dinner for 15 we hosted and celebrating both Hanukkah and Christmas, we attended a conference for new mayors and their spouses at Harvard. It was gracious of the Institute of Politics to extend invitations to mayors' spouses, but aside from the dinner programs, there was nothing relevant for the spouses. I'd been to Boston many times and was adept at navigating. While Rick was in meetings that were expressly focused on new mayors, I took the T from Cambridge to Faneuil Hall Marketplace, had lunch, then walked to the North End. In addition to being known for its bounty of Italian restaurants, one of most historic sites in the country sits in the middle of more than 80 restaurants in the North End. The Old North Church was the first stop on Paul Revere's "Midnight Ride," where he instructed three Boston Patriots to hang two lanterns in the church's steeple on the verge of American Revolutionary War. Before heading back to Cambridge to meet Rick to go to the airport, I made sure to stop at Bova's Bakery for pastries for the kids.

None of the political offices held by Rick compared to running a city of 270,000 residents and overseeing more than 3,000 employees. Rick was an experienced politician. I was a seasoned political spouse. For Jordan and Samuel, their dad had always been elected to something.

In my two-day-old winter white dress, black pumps and chunky green jade necklace, a nod to Rick's campaign color, I shifted my weight from foot to foot in four-inch heels that were already making my feet throb. I felt like the new girl in school, as city staffers and other elected officials greeted us. Steve Couillard and Joe DeLuca were the first plainclothes police officers who would accompany Rick, and sometimes our family, to events. It hadn't occurred to me that Rick would need security in this new job.

The next person I met introduced herself before I had a chance to say, "Nice to meet you." She was all business and uninterested in my extended hand as she gave me her business card and told me to call her if I was stopped for speeding or running a red light. If I was in an accident, I was to call her. She was Assistant Police Chief Melanie Bevan. She looked at Jordan and told me that if she got into even a minor fender bender, we were to call her first.

"Don't call the police," she said. "Call me, and I'll take care of it. You don't want something like that to wind up in the newspaper."

I shoved her card into my purse and continued to stand in place and greet Rick's new staffers. Security for Rick was necessary, but my status as a mayor's spouse didn't seem to warrant special treatment.

From the holding room, we heard singers from local churches performing inspirational songs. Our friend Dave brought Petey, the guide dog we agreed to raise right before the end of the campaign. Petey was a great ice breaker. The deputy mayor's husband and kids fell in love with the golden retriever whose boisterous friendliness covered our dress clothes in dog hair.

When community arts leader Bob Devin Jones took the stage, that was our cue to line up. The officers remained close. Officer Bevan pulled me aside before we went out to greet the crowd. She wanted to schedule a visit to our home to discuss our security system.

"But we have ADT," I said.

She told me that wasn't adequate to protect us. Protect us from what, I wondered?

Rick may have won the election, but he wasn't popular with everyone. The political climate wasn't yet as vitriolic as it would become by the 2016 presidential election, but social media was already fraught with opinions and arguments. Throughout history, politicians have been targeted, threatened and even attacked. The requirement for greater security told me that politicians at any level are susceptible, so I accepted that increased security would be part of our lives for at least the next four years.

A few weeks later, Officer Bevan came to our home to perform a security audit. I'd made coffee and put out a few pastries. I thought I might get to know her, since she was to be my point person in the police department. She wasn't interested.

"Do you own any guns?" she asked.

She looked surprised by my answer.

I told her we did not, but that I had shot bottle targets on my dad's farm as a teenager. No comment. Petey had returned to Southeastern Guide Dogs for advanced training, and we had just welcomed Sunshine, a yellow Labrador. Not even the "First Pup of St. Pete" could evoke a smile.

I drank my coffee and answered questions about whether our window screens had alarms and why we didn't have outside cameras. She took notes as she scrutinized every inch of our 2,700-square-foot home. The only conversation was her suggestions on how to beef up our home security.

Slowly, I began to realize the gravity of being a mayor and what that means for the family. At first, it was hard to be myself around the plainclothes officers who accompanied us to events. Sometimes, I wondered if they were nice to us because it was their job. The more time we spent with them, I realized they were good men. Joe's last name was the same as my father's godfather. We compared family histories and agreed that we weren't related. Steve shared a love of NASCAR with Samuel, a topic of conversation that often came up in the car on the way to events. Finding common ground with the people charged with protecting Rick and our family made it easier to accept what felt like special treatment. When threats were made and Rick warned me that police cruisers would be stationed in front of our home for several days, I knew the security wasn't special treatment. It was necessary.

Still, I wondered about the police officer who sold herself as my personal contact. I wasn't convinced that came with Rick's job as mayor.

That year, Jordan was a sophomore at St. Petersburg High School. Occasionally, fights break out at schools, but that year the fights were more frequent. The International Baccalaureate Program Jordan was enrolled in insulated her from the drama. She rarely mentioned fights when I picked her up at the end of the day. But I knew about them. Officer Bevan had begun texting every time the school took disciplinary action against a student for violence.

The school had a procedure for informing parents when there were lockdowns or other issues. Officer Bevan shared information that the school's administrators didn't disclose with all the parents. It was a burden to know this information and not share it with Jordan. The frequent texts also interfered with work. I spent hours worrying about things I didn't think I needed to know.

Rick and I considered whether we should transfer Jordan from St. Pete High to another school. I investigated alternatives, such as collegiate high school at the local college - dual enrollment that would allow her to remain a St. Pete High student while taking college classes — or virtual school.

I accepted that Rick's job meant that our family received more attention, and that because of that, security was necessary, but the extra attention from this officer because I was the mayor's wife was unpalatable. Rick and I ultimately decided that Jordan would remain at St. Pete High, where she was happy and thriving.

One night, Rick and I were watching television when I received a text from Officer Bevan. When she visited our home for the security audit, she had admonished me about our glass front doors. Despite the thick, black, decorative wrought iron on the outside, anyone could see through the glass.

"I just drove by, and I can see you and Rick sitting on the couch," she texted.

I got up quickly to see the officer speeding toward the end of our street in her unmarked police car. Her texts were bothersome, but the idea that she would drive 15 minutes in the opposite direction of her home to look through our front doors was unnerving.

A few weeks later, I texted her photos of our doors with the privacy film Rick installed. Doorgate was solved, but she continued to text me about seemingly innocuous events at St. Pete High.

Later that year, Jordan tapped the back of a Toyota Camry as she approached a red light. The scratch was barely visible, but the owner understandably wanted to make a claim on our insurance. A few days later, Officer Bevan scolded me for not calling her about the accident when the police department learned that the driver had filed a report.

I'd had enough. I let her know that as Jordan's mother, I'd handled the accident and that I didn't need anyone advising me how to be exempt from being responsible for an accident.

I later learned that Officer Bevan was gunning for the open position of police chief, which Rick needed to fill. She apparently had attached herself to me to try to win my approval, which she assumed would be conveyed to Rick as an endorsement. I stopped responding immediately to her texts. Sometimes I ignored them. The texts stopped when Rick filled the position with another candidate. In 2016, she became chief of police in Bradenton.

I chided myself for not seeing her motives sooner, but we were all adjusting to this new life. I had accepted security and less privacy as part of the package when Rick was elected, so I played along. I vowed not to let someone try to influence me like that again.

I worked to find balance between being guarded but open enough to give people I didn't know the benefit of the doubt. Rick would have this job for at least four years. I didn't want the experience of one officer to sour me.

Much of Rick's first year as mayor was like the first months with a newborn. I was finding my way in a world where some people had given me a title and others expected access because of who my husband was. Rick's position as mayor afforded us opportunities to meet influential people, attend many events and travel.

In the first few months of his term, I was invited to walk in a fashion show, present an award, and sit for an interview with a local paper. Sometimes, the invitations caught us off guard, like when we were told a few minutes before their arrival to an event that Rick and I were to greet Gov. Rick Scott and his wife, Ann. While we waited for them to arrive, I tried to think of what I could say besides hello. During my tenure on the board of the Heart Gallery, I had heard that the Scotts were adoption advocates. Despite our political differences, adoption was a nonpartisan issue. Mrs. Scott and I enjoyed a lovely conversation as we walked them to their table. I was relieved.

Two weeks before Christmas, near the end of Rick's second year as mayor, an invitation for Rick and me arrived via email. It was sent on behalf of another first lady and her husband, the president of the United States. Could we join Barack and Michelle Obama at a White House holiday party?

— Chapter 12 —

CORDIALLY REQUESTING
THE HONOR
OF YOUR PRESENCE

When Rick was first elected to public office, we knew it would mean long days, countless meetings and lots of encounters with constituents. What we didn't anticipate was the mountain of invitations to luncheons, dinners, fundraisers, galas and even restaurant soft openings.

During his years as a City Council member and state legislator, Rick would bring home stacks of invitations. Once a week, we culled through them, calendars in hand, weighing what to accept. Attending evening and weekend events comes with being a politician, but Rick and I agreed that accepting lots of invitations wasn't conducive to a healthy family life.

When Rick became mayor in 2013, the invitations quadrupled. Instead of perusing them together, city staffers vetted them. His public appearances had to be coordinated with his security detail and scheduled around the meetings that filled his 12-hour days. Rick tried to maintain a schedule of no more than four nights out each week.

Most of the time, my name was included on invitations as a courtesy. I carefully chose the events I attended, as I weighed the pros and cons to determine whether an event was worth being absent from our young kids on a school night.

When I did accompany Rick to events, people I didn't know

often stood in line to speak to him. Some interrupted our dinner to speak to him even after the event program had started. The image of people bending down to speak to Rick, their backsides to my face, reminded me of movie characters paying their respects to a don. Accessibility is necessary for a mayor to effectively serve constituents, so I learned not to take it personally when it was obvious people sometimes wanted only to speak to him. Rick always introduced me to the people who knew him. Anyone who wanted to speak to him would also have to say hello to me. I was happy to often play photographer when constituents wanted a selfie with the mayor.

In the beginning, invitations felt like intrusions that took my husband away from me when I wished he were home helping with the kids or sitting next to me on the sofa. When it was clear that Rick wanted to devote most of his working years to public service, I decided to embrace this role. I began to view social events as opportunities to learn something new about our community. I looked forward to finding at least one person with an interesting story. Often, we'd end the evening as friends, promising to follow up at coffee or lunch.

Of all the invitations we received over the years, one stands out – the invitation (sent electronically) from Barack and Michelle Obama to attend a 2015 White House holiday party. We felt like we'd won the lottery.

Rick and I had admired Barack Obama since the first time we met then-Senator Obama on a cold Sunday morning in February 2007. We stood in the driveway of a modern, corner lot home with expansive rounded windows that faced Tampa Bay. We were among a handful of guests who spoke with Obama before he went inside to address the crowd.

By the following February, Obama was a presidential candidate. Spouses are routinely tapped to serve as campaign surrogates, and Michelle Obama was one of the best. It was a rare weeknight when Rick and I were to attend an event at another Tampa home where Mrs. Obama would be campaigning for her husband.

Samuel's fever came on an hour before Rick and I were to walk out the door. It was too late to call a sitter and the grandmothers were unavailable, so I suggested Rick take Jordan instead. She was 9, old enough to stay up past her bedtime on a school night. That night, Michelle Obama politely shook Rick's hand, but she was more interested in talking about American Girl dolls with Jordan, who was the same age as the Obamas' eldest daughter, Malia.

Jordan with Michelle Obama - 2007

Ten years later, when a call went out for memorabilia to be considered for inclusion in the Barack Obama Presidential Center, I sent the photo of Mrs. Obama with her arm around Jordan, and the story of the conversation between two American girls, a future first lady and Jordan.

Shortly after Rick was elected to his first mayoral term, he was invited to join other new mayors at the White House for a roundtable with President Obama. The Oval Office meeting wasn't run by a cabinet staffer. It was Obama who listened when Rick talked about affordable housing and climate change. Like Obama, Rick also had hope. As a new mayor he wanted to reduce poverty, increase equity and create a better life for St. Pete residents.

"He's so real," Rick said.

Rick returned home with a chocolate White House that will never be eaten, matches that will never light a fire and souvenir napkins embossed with the White House seal.

The Obamas' holiday party would be our second visit to the White House as a family. Our first trip in 2007 included a self-guided tour, where 5-year-old Samuel impressed a security guard in the Blue Room who asked him to name another United States president besides Abraham Lincoln who died in office.

Without skipping a beat, Samuel blurted out, "William Henry Harrison."

Still determined to stump him, the security guard asked Samuel what caused President Harrison's death.

"Poon-a-mo-ni-a," Samuel said, correctly identifying the infection of pneumonia that Harrison's doctor and many historians say killed the ninth president after only 32 days in office.

Parent volunteers who'd observed Samuel in his kindergarten classroom would stop me in car line to tell me how Samuel recited the presidents forward and backward. The hard-covered Dorling Kindersley book of presidents with the weathered spine lay next to his bed. Reading and rereading the pages nurtured a natural curiosity for history and politics that had nothing to do with what Rick did for a living.

The only security guards who spoke to us the evening of the White House holiday party were the ones who told us to empty our pockets and purses. Twice they waved their wands over, under and in between. We stood in a long line that weaved like those at Disney. We searched for familiar faces amid the ball gowns that sparkled against business-casual ensembles. There were men in snappy business suits and men in chinos and blazers. I wondered how they came to be invited to a White House holiday party. I surmised that our invitation was the result of Rick's steady support of Obama. He was the first elected Democrat on the west coast of Florida to publicly endorse Obama's first candidacy for president.

We finally got into the hallway that led us to the room where hundreds of partygoers were already gathered. Tuxedoed waiters milled through the crowd offering champagne. We ran into Rick's 2013 campaign manager, Cesar Fernandez, and his fiancé, Ailyn, who already had their Champagne. Behind the main room was a long rectangular room with several tables. The platters of shrimp, filet mignon, cheeses, fruit and the best macaroni and cheese I would ever eat hadn't yet arrived. White and milk chocolate replicas of the White House, ice cream sundae stations, cheesecake platters and candy lined the perimeter of the room.

We postponed our Champagne for four front-row spots across from a lonely lectern that stood like a wallflower waiting for a dance partner. I was sure that's where the Obamas would stand when they addressed the crowd. My toes, which had been shoved into rarely worn black patent leather pumps, barked angrily while we waited for the hosts. I thought about the front-row seat I'd had to Rick's political career and how it led us to the ones we had that evening.

"Make friends with your neighbors," the man from Obama's security team suggested as he proceeded down the line repeating the same instructions every three feet. Without taking a breath, he recited how we all could get a picture with the Obamas.

"No selfies with the president," he warned.

We were to give our cell phones to the person on our left. They would take our photo with the Obamas. Our new friends would return our phones and give us theirs. We would snap their pictures. A memorable and historical party favor for sure.

After about 90 minutes, the crowd grew silent. "Hail to the Chief" played, and the Obamas descended the grand staircase to join the lonely lectern that was now the center of attention.

We were only about a hundred feet from them. President Obama speaks as if the words are meant only for you. He seemed to lock eyes with every individual in the room. His jokes made us laugh, but his words inspired. We had no idea how much we would miss his calming and intellectual oratory once he left office.

With Michelle Obama at the White House Holiday Party - 2015

That year, the Obamas hosted 20 holiday receptions at the White House. I'll bet Michelle Obama could tell me about sore feet, but I forgot about mine as we strolled the White House halls. The Christmas tree dedicated to military families, each ornament a service member's story, brought tears to my eyes. The life-sized replicas of Bo and Sunny reminded us of our Labradors. Vanderbilt University's acapella group, The Melodores, drew crowds as they sang beautiful holiday songs.

If Rick hadn't said yes to running for the City Council in 1999, we would've probably spent that Friday evening falling asleep to Netflix. Instead, Rick and Samuel got high fives from the president and Jordan and I got one of Michelle Obama's famous hugs. It felt like a reunion with old friends.

Nothing lasts forever, and the political bubble eventually pops. Politics has brought challenges that we would not have had if Rick had continued running his law practice. But this life has also provided gifts. The physical ones, tokens of appreciation and awards, usually end up in Rick's City Hall office.

Gifts of experiences live in my heart and in relationships I have with people I might have never met if I wasn't a political spouse. That has left me humbled, inspired and grateful.

Michelle Obama's life changed because of her husband's job, but it didn't change who she was. She is married to a man who was the most powerful person in the world for eight years. She had been a political spouse for 18 years, but that night in 2008 when she spent a few moments talking to a little girl about dolls, she was a mom.

Long evenings picking at chicken dinners, standing next to Rick while others lobbied him, or waiting at home while he advanced his career led to one of the most treasured evenings of my life. I am grateful to have been invited to the White House holiday party. I am also glad I listened to my teachers' advice. Always pick a seat in the front of the room. That's where the best stuff happens.

— Chapter 13 —

ON-THE-JOB TRAINING

When Rick became mayor, I didn't realize rappelling 28 stories down the Bank of America building in St. Pete would be one of the many events on his calendar.

The invitation from Big Brothers and Big Sisters of Tampa Bay was a fundraiser for their programs. Rick showed up that afternoon, got a brief lesson in how to hold the rope and not bounce off the side of the building with his feet. The kids and I sat on the curb across the street and craned our necks toward the sky while he was coached by a professional on how to safely descend.

Members of the media joked about wills and life insurance while I tried not to worry. I trusted the experienced professionals wouldn't let him fall. He looked confident from hundreds of feet away, but I wondered who thought this would be a good idea and why Rick didn't say no. In his defense, this was early in his first term, and requests were flying in faster than his new staff could handle. I don't think even Rick was fully apprised of what this adventure would entail. We cheered when his feet touched the ground, then toasted with a beer with fellow rappeler Terry Tomalin, the outdoors adventurer and husband of Rick's deputy mayor, Dr. Kanika Tomalin.

If watching my husband rappel down the tallest building in the city didn't take my breath away, a dinner at the home of a four-star general might have. Rick sold me on accepting an invitation to dinner with Gen. Lloyd Austin and his wife, Charlene. Rick had previously met Gen. Austin. I hadn't met either the general or his wife.

Austin, now U.S. secretary of defense, had been commander

of Central Command (CENTCOM) at MacDill Air Force Base in Tampa for just over a year when Rick began his first mayoral term.

CENTCOM is headquarters to the U.S. military forces that protect American security interests in 20 countries from the Horn of Africa to Central Asia, including Iraq, Iran, Pakistan, Afghanistan, the Arabian Peninsula and the northern Red Sea and the five republics of Central Asia.

When we arrived and saw cars lining both sides of the street, I wondered if we were at the wrong address. The invitation implied it was a dinner for us and the Austins. Gen. and Mrs. Austin gave us a brief tour of their home before introducing us to a few couples on the way to the dining room with an oval table set for 20. Rick and I searched for our names on the place cards. Mine was on one side of the table, and his was across from me and to the left.

This wasn't what I'd envisioned when we agreed to attend this dinner. I'd exchanged no more than pleasantries with the general and his wife. Now, I was seated between two men I'd never met.

Gen. Austin welcomed everyone, then gave a synopsis of his career and his goals during his tenure at MacDill. Before the courses began, he asked us all to introduce ourselves, moving counterclockwise around the table. I was relieved to be seated at the opposite end of the general, which meant that 12 speakers would go before me. Every one of them recited long and impressive resumes with colorful experiences to match. The guest on my right was a former ambassador who is a big GOP donor, the guest on my left a CEO with businesses throughout the world. Even the spouses of the uber successful people at that dinner had lengthy resumes. I was a former stay-at-home mom who worked part time for a local nonprofit organization.

Each time someone finished speaking, my heart pounded. I tried to inconspicuously take deep breaths. I sipped water to quench my dry mouth, which felt like sandpaper.

I rehearsed several versions of what I might say about myself, my background or my job that might be relevant to our hosts. Nothing I came up with could compare to the important things that everyone in that room had done. Then it came to me, like a name you remember only when it wakes you from a deep sleep.

So far, no one in that room had mentioned working with veterans, an important segment of the military. I opened with my rare status as a St. Pete native, my service on the boards of organizations whose work benefitted families and children, and my job as a public relations manager for a nonprofit that serves adults with disabilities. My heart still fluttered, but no one seemed to notice as I recounted how my work as a volunteer puppy raiser for Southeastern Guide Dogs changes lives. I described how some of the dogs that don't become guides help veterans who suffer from PTSD. I got to help someone I'd never met by loving and training a puppy for a year, then returning it to the organization for advanced skills training.

I regretted not having business cards with me when a few of the guests asked for information about Southeastern. I vowed to be better prepared in the future. I left the Austins' home that evening knowing that a long resume of accomplishments and accolades isn't proof of meaningful work. Practice doesn't always make perfect, but it made me more comfortable and ready for the next time I would find myself in a precarious situation.

A few months later, I threw on the brown lace overlay dress I'd worn a few months earlier on election night to attend a dinner for the Poynter Institute's Edward R. Murrow Program for Journalists where national television journalist Dan Rather was the keynote speaker. Rick and I met Rather in the lobby before the event. I wish I had a copy of the photograph that ran in the *Tampa Bay Times* that weekend.

It would've been enough to meet the iconic journalist, but when we were shown to our table, there was Rather, seated with Paul Tash, the Times' chairman and CEO. Tash, whom I've known for decades because I once worked for the paper, motioned for me to sit next to Rather. Rick sat on the other side of me.

Before dinner was served, Tash put Rick in the hot seat as he questioned him about some of his recent decisions as mayor. Rick was trying to maneuver his way out of the awkward conversation when Rather told Tash to leave him alone and let him enjoy his dinner. I spent the rest of the evening answering Rather's questions about the history of St. Pete, while he talked with us about the state of the media in the 21st century and how much it had changed since the era of Edward R. Murrow and other broadcast news pioneers.

I began to view each opportunity as St. Petersburg's first lady as a once-in-a-lifetime moment, and soon there was another. Our family traveled on a chartered plane to Havana, Cuba, with the Tampa Bay Rays' owners and executives and their families.

With Dan Rather - 2016

We were part of the delegation to Havana for a 2016 exhibition game between the Rays and the Cuba national baseball team. Major League Baseball and the Cuban Baseball Federation commissioned the game to spotlight the need for a system that would permit Cuban players to come to the United States more freely.

President Barack Obama, his wife, Michelle, and daughters, Maliá and Sasha, were also in Cuba to attend the game as guests of Cuban President Raul Castro. Obama was the first president since Calvin Coolidge in 1928 to visit Cuba. In December 2014, Obama and Castro announced the beginning of the process of normalizing relations between Cuba and the United States. The landmark game between the Rays and Cuban national team would be part of that process.

When we arrived in Havana, we were shuttled to the Melia Cohiba Hotel, a modern restored hotel where the baseball players also were staying. We were welcomed with mojitos and a spread of meats, fruits and desserts. Rick had been to Cuba once, so he was eager to make our first visit as a family memorable.

Shortly after checking into our room, we went for a walk. Rick wore his Rays ball cap, which attracted attention from a few of the Cuban people who shouted to us from open windows in their homes. Some of them followed us as we walked through Old Havana. One man invited us into his home, where a young child was sitting in a small, plastic swimming pool, trying to stay cool. From his gestures, we thought he was asking for money. When we offered him pesos, he refused, and led us down the street to his friend's restaurant. He led us down a long hallway with tiled walls that told the story of the Cuban Revolution through images of

Fidel Castro and Fulgencio Batista, the dictator Castro opposed. He brought us to his friend's restaurant and insisted we eat. It was mid-afternoon, and we had a scheduled dinner with the rest of the delegation that evening, so we settled on Cuban coffee and a light snack. That made him happy.

The next day we explored Old Havana; ate lunch at the La Ghiradella paladar, a private non-government-owned restaurant; sipped daquiris at El Floridita, where the daquiri was born; and people-watched on the Malecon, a historic boulevard along the seawall. Jordan was interviewed by Craig Patrick of Fox 13 Tampa Bay for a teen's perspective on Cuba.

I photographed as much as I could – the stray dogs that looked healthy and well-fed, the friendly people who said hello to us on the streets, the brightly-colored 1950s cars, the art nouveau and art deco architecture, a synagogue, and a boxing gym that was closed to the public. The Cuban people knew we weren't regular tourists. The Tampa Bay Rays baseball cap Rick wore was a conversation starter with people we met in the streets. Eventually, Rick gave his cap to a Cuban baseball fan.

*The Kriseman Family at the Tampa Bay Rays-Cuban National
Team Exhibition Game, Havana, Cuba, 2016*

The night before the baseball game we joined players, team executives and the rest of the delegation at La Divina Pastore Restaurante. Mojitos, hand-rolled cigars and musicians playing Cuban music were in every corner. Vintage cars were dispersed throughout the property. The players enjoyed posing on the cars, cigars dangling from their lips, cheesing for the camera.

We'd heard a rumor that Jimmy Buffett would be arriving from Miami on his boat to play a surprise concert. We got some drinks and found spots near the stage while we waited for word that Buffett had arrived.

Rick and I have met Buffett a few times. We used to be members of the Tampa Bay Parrot Head Club. Jordan was a Parakeet when she was little, a distinction reserved for the youngest Parrot Heads. You could say we're die-hard fans who rarely miss a Buffett concert. In 2010, when Rick was in the state House, he drove from Tallahassee to the Florida Amphitheater to present Buffett with a proclamation to honor his impact on the state and his work throughout Florida on manatee conservation. The kids and I drove from St. Pete to meet Rick. When we walked in, Buffett and his band were rehearsing "Floridays." After they finished that song, we met Buffett and Rick read the proclamation to him while Elvis, the guide dog puppy we were training, licked Buffett's shorts. Buffett was unfazed. We posed for pictures before receiving a backstage tour and watching him and his Coral Reefer band rehearse for the next day's concert.

In Havana, Cuba, at a private concert with Jimmy Buffett

Now six years later, we'd be up close again as Buffett sang about "Havana Daydreamin'" *in* Havana! I was close enough to the stage to pick up his song list when it fell from his pedestal.

There were others from Tampa who'd traveled to Havana. They were part of the group that has worked for years to restore relations between Tampa and Havana. One of them knew Fidel Castro and his family, and he told Rick and me that there might be an opportunity to meet him. It was no secret that Castro's health was shaky, so I wasn't convinced we would get the chance, but I was hopeful. I'd met Presidents Clinton and Obama, Ringo Starr and even Kiss front man Gene Simmons, but I'd never met a dictator.

I didn't meet him after all, but I did meet one of his nephews. I tried to remember the Spanish I'd learned in high school and college but hadn't used in years. That didn't matter when Rick was whisked away into a private room while I was left waiting with Jordan and Samuel. A quick handshake with the dictator's nephew was as far as it would go. Passing through the thick, carved wood door was for men only. While we waited for Rick, the kids and I walked around the party. It was fun watching the Rays players sit on the back of convertible 1950s pastel-colored cars as they posed for photos. I grabbed a few more souvenir cigars before we bumped into *Tampa Bay Times* baseball writer Marc Topkin, whom I'd known for years.

Ever since the first special events we attended when Rick was on the City Council and throughout the state House days when we got a VIP tour of the Wizarding World of Harry Potter, I told myself to never get used to or expect the special treatment. Not even when we watched the space shuttle lift off at Cape Canaveral in a room filled with astronauts and politicians. Access to events like these come with the job, but someday it will end. My mantra was to be grateful and glad for the experiences.

Not all of Rick's first term was a party. The perks are bright spots that make the hard times tolerable. Life guarantees that there will always be hard times, but we hope they're few and short-lived.

The stormy Saturday afternoon in August 2015 when Rick received a phone call from his communications director, Ben Kirby, was the beginning of a saga that would threaten to upend his political career and negate the mostly positive moments we'd experienced as a political couple and family.

Summer storms are common in St. Pete. Most people who buy homes in the low-lying neighborhoods know they will sometimes flood. It's the tradeoff for living near the water. That month, storms were far heavier than normal, which overwhelmed the city's aged wastewater system.

Rick had to choose between discharging partially treated wastewater into the bay or having raw sewage flow down some city streets and into homes. He chose discharging into the bay. Before the storm event, Rick had consulted the staffers in charge of the system, who assured him that everything was operating optimally. *Creative Loafing* was the first to disclose the news of the discharge, which quickly spiraled into a blame game. No matter who runs a city department, the buck stops with the mayor. It didn't matter that the staffers in charge of the wastewater system withheld vital information about the aging, failing sewer system. It was Rick who was blamed when the excessive rain caused wastewater discharges.

It was hard for me to read reporters' incomplete versions of stories. This wasn't the same newspaper I'd worked for years ago. Infrastructure had been ignored by at least four mayors and dozens of city officials before him, but the newspaper chose to portray Rick as the one to blame. The bill had come due for a problem that had been ignored for decades. No matter what led to the problem, it was Rick's job to fix it.

If social media were judge and jury, Rick would've been convicted and hanged.

The debate over fault and the eagerness to blame Rick for the system's failing created a political climate in the city that would lead Rick into the biggest fight of his political life.

The honeymoon of his first term was over. Rick's legacy hinged on fixing this problem for the long term, not the Band-Aid temporary fixes from leaders before him. While he searched for a solution, he continued to be a mayor who implemented a generous family leave policy, gave all employees an extra day off each year, attracted new businesses, persevered to build a new pier, and worked to build equity throughout the city.

I listened as Rick searched for answers to his staffers' betrayal. I listened to his strategy for fixing the problems so future mayors wouldn't have to. Together, we fought against lies that circulated in political circles about his role in the system's failure. If someone asked me about sewage, I told them the truth. It wasn't Rick's fault, but it was his responsibility, and he would fix the problem.

Reporters continued to cover the story through the summer of 2016. Rick and I needed a break from the battering he was taking in the public sphere. That August, after we moved Jordan to college and got Samuel settled into his final year of middle school, we began to plan.

A break would come soon, in 2017, for our 25th anniversary.

— Chapter 14 —

ALWAYS TAKE THE TRIP

I carefully folded the $588 check into a sheet of white paper so it couldn't be seen through the envelope. The final payment secured our reservation at Casa Amore, a thousand-year-old villa in the Tuscan village of San Sano, Italy, population 82.

Our 25th anniversary trip was a celebration and a family vacation. Rick and I looked forward to the countryside, landmarks, art and history. We also looked forward to drinking sulfite-free red wine that wouldn't leave us longing for an afternoon nap.

Jordan was studying art history at the University of Florida. The art she'd seen in books would soon be at her fingertips when we visited the Uffizi and Accademia Galleries. Samuel's reward for enduring museums, the Vatican and the Sistine Chapel, would be a visit to the Ferrari Museum in Modena.

Most of all, I looked forward to visiting the country of my paternal grandfather. Joseph Nicolosi was 3 when he sailed with his uncles from Catania, Sicily, in 1911. They landed in the Lower East Side in New York before joining other Italian immigrants in Lawrence, Massachusetts.

Joe and my grandmother, Anne, traveled between St. Pete and Lawrence yearly after my Aunt Frances was born in 1939. By 1949, they were full-time residents of St. Pete. My grandmother was a nurse on the obstetrics and gynecology floor at St. Anthony's Hospital, an eight-block walk from their home in the Euclid-St. Paul neighborhood. My grandfather was a barber and installer of linoleum flooring. His band, Joe Nichols and His Musical Pennies, played Knights of Columbus events, private parties, concerts in the bandshell at Williams Park, the St. Petersburg Symphony, and the Florida Philharmonic. The band was often broadcast live from St. Petersburg Municipal Pier on WSUN, which stood for "Why Stay Up North," the first television station in the Tampa Bay market.

Summers were spent in Salisbury Beach, Massachusetts, five miles from the New Hampshire border. Teens' preference to socialize with their peers was as strong in the 1950s as it is today. Dad and Aunt Frances resented being pulled out of school a month before summer dismissal to travel north to help their parents ready their summer cottages for tenants. My grandparents managed three cottages while they spent the entire summer in the small resort town about an hour north of Boston with two amusement parks, a boardwalk with kitschy shops, walkup stands with fried clams, pizza, ice cream and other sweets. They remained past Labor Day, after the last of the tenants checked out, which meant that Dad and Aunt Frances always started a new school year late.

The tradition of helping in the family pet products business was passed on to my brother, Steve, and me. We spent many of our summers in an unairconditioned warehouse learning how to screen print, fill shampoo bottles, and build boxes to ship products. I drove a forklift before I had a driver's license. We earned as much as the other employees, which was a consolation to me when I missed hanging out with friends at the beach.

Dad was a self-made man, and he liked being the captain of his ship. His 1973 Jeep Grand Cherokee blared county music whether we liked it or not. He navigated family road trips through 13 states on the Eastern Seaboard, and to Graceland in Memphis so my brother and I could see Elvis' pink Cadillac on the way to my mom's birthplace of Stuttgart, Arkansas.

Traveling was a way for me to spend time with my parents, who often worked long hours and on weekends. In the decade before he died at 66, my dad spent weekends at Lake Cumberland, Kentucky, a few hours from his farm. He could back his 100-foot-long houseboat out of the slip, one hand on the wheel and the other gesturing as he spoke, always a Salem Light dangling from his lips.

I grew up hearing the stories of my Aunt Frances' travels to Egypt, Italy, Guatemala, Spain, England and other countries. At 49, the only countries I'd visited were Jamaica, the Bahamas and Canada. Our trip to Italy would fulfill the desire to travel that was born from hours spent looking at my grandmother's photo albums.

Steve and I spent afternoons after school at my grandparents' house. Nanu and Nana, shortened from the Italian Nonno and Nonna, lived down the street from us and just three blocks from St. Paul Catholic School. Often, we arrived to see Nanu and his friends drinking screwdrivers and puffing on Hav-A-Tampas while they played pinochle. If their snowbird friends were visiting, we were invited to join them for dinner around the canary yellow Formica and chrome dining room table.

While the adults enjoyed coffee, dessert and conversations that lingered past our bedtimes, Steve watched television while I looked at Nana's photo albums from my grandfather's recliner. Nana organized photos of their toy Manchester terriers, my dad, Aunt Frances, my parents' 1965 wedding, Expo 67 in Montreal and vacations to Germany, Switzerland and, of course, Italy. I carefully peeled back the cellophane from the album pages to read the location, date and names that my grandmother wrote in perfect cursive on the back of each photo.

When Nana was moved to a nursing home in 2001, I happily inherited the photo albums. Our family was still writing its story when she died March 26, 2002. Jordan was 4, but she knew her great-grandmother from our weekly visits and grocery shopping excursions. I would place Jordan in the cart, her legs dangling through the leg holes. Nana pushed the cart while Jordan held her grocery list, which was always written in neat cursive on the back of an envelope. Later that year, we adopted Samuel. He knows her through the stories we tell, like the birthday dinners of Stouffer's lasagna and Sara Lee freezer cakes with gifts of hand lotion for the women, soap on a rope for the guys, and $10 checks.

Rick and I had been dating for seven months when Nana gave him a birthday card with a dark-haired man in a three-piece suit holding a briefcase. The cover read, "Celebrate your birthday like a lawyer." Inside: "Debrief yourself and uphold your penal system."

She bought the card because it said "lawyer," and Rick was a lawyer. We saved the card for years and still tell that story. Retelling family stories honors the memory of those who've died and provides a glimpse of who they were for the ones who never met them. Seeing where they came from only deepens the connection.

Although Rick shares my love of travel, long vacations were rare early in our marriage. Rick was the sole practitioner in his law office, so where we traveled and for how long depended on client demands and how much money was in the bank.

After Jordan was born in 1997, we went to Atlanta every three months to see Rick's mom before dementia and Alzheimer's disease robbed her of her memory. We were stealing time to give our kids a chance to make memories with their grandmother.

I wanted to create the kind of memories for our kids that I had from childhood trips and stories of the people I never met in my grandmother's photos.

Four months before our anniversary trip, Rick launched his reelection campaign. Stepping back into the ring, even as an incumbent, is like reintroducing yourself to old friends.

St. Petersburg's progressive political climate attracts multiple candidates for every office. By March 2017, Rick had three opponents. None of them presented a serious challenge to an incumbent with many accomplishments, money in the bank and a long list of endorsements and supporters.

Perennial candidate Paul Congemi was known for disruption and bigotry. He was banned from Kentucky Fried Chicken after cursing at employees. We were confident he couldn't earn enough votes to be mayor. Who would cut the ribbon should a new KFC open in St. Pete?

African People's Socialist Party activist Jesse Nevel ran on a platform calling for reparations and outlawing gentrification. He accused Rick of being a criminal and for being responsible for the city's sewage issues, an inherited problem he fixed during his first term.

Anthony Cates was a passionate businessman and father. During debates, he emphasized that he was running to make his father proud. I wondered whether he really wanted the job since he often complimented Rick.

These candidates didn't appear to pose a reelection threat, but Rick took nothing for granted. He hired Jacob Smith, his 2013 field organizer, as campaign manager.

On a Sunday morning in April, we met Jacob, new field director Adrienne Bogen, and John Rowley and his film crew in front of my childhood home. The team chose the 1924 colonial that my parents bought for $15,000 in 1973 on a block with hexagonal sidewalks under canopied oaks as the setting for Rick's first commercial of the 2017 campaign.

For hours, Rick walked toward the camera, dressed in a suit, and recited the script.

"I know we can keep St. Pete moving forward," he said.

Over and over, until it was perfect.

This was John's fourth political campaign for Rick. We could enjoy a beer with him and rely on him to be honest with us when it came to how Rick should campaign. The willingness to listen to your consultants can be the difference between winning and losing.

After filming, John, Rick and I caught up over drinks at Hawthorne Bottle Shoppe. Jacob had been silent when we mentioned the trip, which was three months before the August primary. We sought approval, so we told John we were going to Italy for two weeks.

"Do you think that's a problem?" I asked.

John's poker face was so good he could've won a game of Texas hold'em with a 2 and a 7. We were his clients; he wasn't paid to police our personal lives.

"It's only two weeks," I said. "Rick will work hard before we leave and even harder when we return."

John and Jacob remained neutral while we continued to make plans. Three weeks before our trip we had lunch with Ron and Sherry Sacino, the owners of the Tuscan villa where we would spend part of the trip. Over tuna melts at Central Oyster Bar, they told us the best places to eat, which vineyards to visit, and where to buy olive oil, attend Catholic Mass, get groceries, and take cooking classes.

Midway through lunch, Rick got a text.

Rick Baker, who had been mayor from 2000 to 2009, was at City Hall. The rumor was true. He was filing to run against Rick.

St. Petersburg's charter prevents mayors from serving more than two consecutive terms, but they can serve again after a break. Money doesn't make one powerful but being the top dog in city politics can. Even though Baker earned more than twice the mayor's salary in his post-mayor private life, he wanted his old job back.

That night, John texted me:

"A new phase."

The next day, the campaign strategy changed. The ad filmed a few weeks earlier would air sooner. Fundraising became the focus. Campaign staffers were added to expand field operations.

Baker launched his campaign via Facebook Live on the City Hall steps with dozens of supporters surrounding him. He shook his finger as he vowed to take the city back.

He warned that if Rick served another term St. Petersburg would be unrecognizable, in financial ruin and riddled with crime. Rick's record of accomplishments in less than four years proved the opposite, but Donald Trump's 2016 victory showed that the truth sometimes doesn't matter much.

Rick's job was on the line, and our anniversary trip was suddenly in jeopardy. If a candidate earned 50% of the votes plus 1 in the August primary, the election would be over. Baker wanted to knock Rick out in the first round.

We worried that being gone for two weeks would hurt the campaign. We considered shortening the trip, but that didn't solve the problem of an absent incumbent in the middle of a contentious election. We didn't have an answer, but I knew Rick and I wouldn't forgive ourselves if we took the trip and he lost the election.

Cash is king in political campaigns, with advertising being a campaign's biggest expense. Two weeks without fundraising could financially devastate the campaign. There were no debates planned during the time we would be gone, so unless someone told the media, Rick's absence probably wouldn't be noticed.

We ping-ponged between celebrating a milestone anniversary or a second term. The decision was ours, but we wanted the blessing of Rick's campaign team.

We sought the counsel of family members, Rick's chief of staff, and a few friends. We asked John again. There was no poker face this time, only his voice on speaker. He told us not to go.

Since Rick entered politics in 1999, I've learned to live with frequent disruptions or amendments to our schedule. Sometimes, I had been lonely when Rick commuted to Tallahassee, but I had adjusted to being a political spouse. Public life was no longer the burden it seemed to be in the early years. I didn't mind being called first lady, even when the police cars stationed in front our home left me unsettled. I accepted that Rick's passion for politics wasn't a phase, but there were limits to what I would tolerate. The thought of forsaking our dream vacation and anniversary celebration because of Rick's job was infuriating.

I thought about my friends who didn't have to seek others' opinions when they wanted to travel. Their lives weren't planned around political campaigns.

Would supporters still vote for Rick if they knew he left town for two weeks in the middle of a campaign? If his absence were due to a family emergency, voters could forgive him. But a trip to

Europe could be considered frivolous. The opposition ads were already written in my head.

Rick wanted to serve the people of St. Petersburg for four more years. All we wanted was two weeks in Italy. A job ends, but relationships remain. I've always told Rick that when he's finished with politics, the kids and I will be what he has left. If people didn't vote for him because he took a two-week vacation, then he wasn't meant to be mayor.

Two days before our scheduled flight to Rome, we were still paralyzed with indecision. Rick's campaign was focused on moving forward, but I couldn't even get the suitcases down from the garage shelves.

Time was running out when Rick suggested consulting an ex-mayor of another Tampa Bay city.

Pam Iorio was a former Tampa mayor who was also married with a son and a daughter. Rick often worked with her husband, who was the Pinellas County administrator. Of all the people we consulted, her family most closely mirrored ours. None of the family members, friends, campaign staffers or consultants we asked had ever been a mayor up for reelection during a contentious campaign.

With her permission, Rick put her on the speaker so I could hear the conversation. She echoed my words about the importance of family as she talked of life after public service. He would never get these days back, she told him. She urged him not to squander an opportunity to celebrate 25 years with his soulmate.

Jacob and John were incredulous, but we'd made our decision. While we were gone, the team mobilized volunteers, called voters, canvassed neighborhoods, and created digital ads for social media.

Rick came through on his promise to use the five-hour time difference to his advantage. Each night after we returned from dinner, Rick sat on the stone wall a couple of hundred feet from our villa and made fundraising calls. It was the only spot with cell phone service.

Each morning, we checked social media, expecting to find a story about our trip. We later learned that Peter Schorsch, an influential political blogger who was often critical of Rick and friendly with the former mayor, knew about the trip but kept it to himself. His silence was another anniversary gift.

Rick campaigning in Italy - 2017

The right path isn't always the straightest or the easiest. Like marriage, our decision to go to Italy was a leap of faith. Faith in Rick that the voters of St. Petersburg still wanted him around to finish the job he started. Faith that our campaign team would keep things running while we were gone. And faith in ourselves that we made the right decision.

If anyone ever seeks my counsel when faced with a decision like this, I will always tell them: Put family first and take the trip.

Chapter 15

LOST IN DEBATE

I parked my white Hyundai Santa Fe in one of the few empty spots. By now, I knew the drill. Showing up was the easy part. Much like rote sequences at the gym – cardio, legs, then arms – political exercises were second nature: Find my center of calm. Banish the butterflies. Breathe in, breathe out. Pray. Repeat.

Years of political campaigns had brought us to this evening, the second debate between Rick and five other candidates running for mayor. Like the sound of musical notes intensifying as they lead to a crescendo, this evening would be a key point in a campaign that was just getting started. This was Rick's eighth political campaign, but nothing could have prepared me for the showdown brewing inside the ballroom of the Hilton St. Petersburg Bayfront.

Since the day former Mayor Rick Baker entered the race, I struggled to mute the negativity that pervaded conversations, social media and the news. To others, I appeared confident and calm, a tenacious political spouse. Inside, I felt like Fred from *The Flintstones* when angel and devil whisper good thoughts versus bad thoughts into his ear that leave him conflicted. I struggled to contain my angst and worry while Rick battled for a second term.

At the first mayoral debate at a local church a week earlier, candidates had stacked the audience with supporters who cheered and jeered while Baker and another candidate, Jesse Nevel, leveled accusations against Rick.

After that night, I thought I was ready for anything, but I prayed I wouldn't see a repeat of that first debate.

As I strode through the lobby of the Hilton with my mom, Jordan and Samuel, I tried to look confident but not too cocky. I looked for Rick. I wanted to give him one more hug and kiss. I saw him through the sliver of the cracked-open door of the holding room with the other candidates and their campaign staffs. Instead of walking in and taking the chance I might come face-to-face with Baker, I texted him good luck and went to find seats in the standing-room-only ballroom.

Each candidate's camp had staked out its territory, much like soldiers on a battlefield. I wondered which side would fire first. I made nervous small talk with friends and supporters who approached me.

The red-shirted folks who belonged to the Baker camp sat on the right. Behind them were a group of boisterous 20-somethings who supported Nevel, the Uhurus' candidate. Rick's supporters were sprinkled throughout the room. A typical teen, Samuel bolted to the rear of the ballroom to watch with his college-age golf friends who worked for the campaign.

A volunteer on the campaign and the mother of one of the golf friends motioned to us. She had three seats on the left side of the room, away from the opposition. I felt cocooned, safe from the negativity that pervaded the room. I looked around and saw several uniformed police officers.

I wondered whether this debate would erupt into angry shouts from the Uhurus, whose M.O. was to create the kind of loud distractions that had shut down the City Council candidate debate a few minutes earlier.

I repeated my mantra to myself: Breathe in. Breathe out. Banish those angry wasps.

Baker wasn't Rick's only opponent, but as a popular former mayor who was still well-known to many, he was Rick's biggest threat. When he reentered the bloody boxing ring of local politics, he wasted no time throwing the first of many punches. He hoped to achieve at least a 50% +1 vote margin in the Aug. 29 primary, a knockout that would send my husband packing.

Other candidates included Momma Tee Lassiter, a community activist; Nevel, the African Socialist Party's candidate; and Anthony Cates, a businessman who was running to make his father proud. A sixth candidate, who had been disqualified, also attended. Paul Congemi, a homophobic born-again Christian who had been banned from a local Kentucky Fried Chicken, did not attend.

Most of the people in the room knew there was only one opponent for Rick: The other Rick, the former mayor.

I avoided looking at the Baker family that evening. They were now opponents, not the friends we thought we had been when Baker was mayor and Rick was a City Council member. Joyce Baker and I had bonded over shared interests and even some similar life paths. We both held leadership roles in the Junior League. Our kids were close in age and often hung out together at city events. We even shared the bond of being adoptive parents. Now, our Ricks were opponents in a campaign that had become nasty before it even commenced.

There had been rumblings for the past year that Baker was being recruited to run for a third term. He wanted his old job back, so he canvassed neighborhoods to ask residents whether they were happy with the direction of the city. He not-so-quietly lobbied supporters behind the scenes as he tried to gauge his popularity among voters.

It would have been hypocritical for Joyce and me to embrace as old friends, make small talk and ignore the elephant in the room that was this ugly campaign.

A palpable tenseness pervaded the room. Voice levels rose. I felt like the reporters in the room were watching me as they waited for candidate introductions to begin.

Almost immediately, the debate erupted into a shouting match, with most of the shouts, jeers and chants coming from the Uhurus. The sponsors ended it 37 minutes later, the *Tampa Bay Times* reported, after the forum "degenerated into a pushing, screaming scrum" that brought "a stream of police officers" to the ballroom.

"Reparations!" the Uhurus screamed, over and over. Nevel represented their quest for financial compensation for the Black community as punishment for years of inequity. Rick was not responsible for the racism and inequity that had pervaded St. Pete for most of its history. The Uhurus called him a racist, liar and criminal anyway.

Like many communities, St. Petersburg had a lot of work to do to right decades of systemic wrong and erase generational poverty. It did not matter that much *had* changed over the years, and that Rick's administration could cite tangible gains toward increasing equity, jobs and economic development in the African American community.

The Uhurus seemed to have one goal that evening: create a disturbance that would scuttle any semblance of an informative debate. A look at the Uhurus' social media accounts told me that their goal that evening was to capture sound bites and video that buttressed their national campaign for reparations.

The moderators tried in vain to ask the candidates questions. Each time a candidate tried to answer, they were quickly shouted down with accusations and name calling. When the debate organizers called a halt and asked the crowd to leave, there was more shouting and fisticuffs, and police had to disperse the angry mob.

My mom, Jordan and I ping-ponged between exiting toward the front, where the candidates were, or going to the back to find Samuel. I couldn't see Samuel. I trusted he was safe with the campaign staffers, so we pushed our way through the crowd to get to Rick. As we moved toward the front, I saw Joyce Baker. Our eyes spoke what words could not utter. We were fearful, frustrated and maybe even a little sad after witnessing the ugly debacle.

I kept looking back for my mom, who momentarily disappeared, when I heard a voice ask me, "Are you okay? Do you need me to find Steve?"

It was Joyce. She was referring to Steve Couillard, one of the St. Petersburg police officers assigned to our family after Rick was elected.

Joyce and I hadn't spoken in years. This campaign had quickly created factions among groups of friends and supporters throughout the city. Mutual friends and acquaintances had already picked which Rick they were supporting. Divisive negativity between the two camps was fueled on social media, in the media, in local businesses and among social circles. I wondered if any affection we had for each other as community volunteers, moms and campaign spouses still existed now that her husband was aggressively competing for my husband's job.

The exchange between Joyce and me provided a moment of humanity between opponents' wives. It plucked me out of my angst and resentment over her husband's candidacy. For a moment, Joyce and I connected over shared distress, a reminder that we are all human.

Samuel still had not found us, but he was a big kid, almost 6 feet tall, and was with college juniors who knew how to take care of themselves. Soon, Joe DeLuca, our other security officer, brought him to us in the hallway where were waited with the other candidates until the protesters were gone.

Never in my life could I have imagined I would be embroiled

in a scenario where political tempers rivaled July temperatures.

Some political spouses would've called it quits after a frightening night like that. The next debate was in 15 days. We had two weeks to muster the resolve to prepare for more attacks against Rick's record while people we thought were friends supported Baker. To avoid the kind of disturbance that had occurred at the Hilton, the debate sponsors, the *Tampa Bay Times* and Bay News 9, invited only the candidates they deemed the top two contenders: my Rick and Rick Baker.

On the way to the Palladium Theater that night, we blasted Pit Bull's "Fireball" before playing what would become Rick's anthem for the 2017 campaign, Tom Petty's "I Won't Back Down."

Kriseman Family walking into the Palladium Theatre - July 2017 -
Tampa Bay Times, photographer Dirk Shadd

Rick was confident that he could defeat Baker in a one-on-one debate. We left Rick's black city-issued SUV and walked toward the Palladium in the blinding sun. *Tampa Bay Times* photographer Dirk Shadd snapped a photo that captured our sentiment: We were ready for battle, even if you couldn't see it in our eyes that were shielded by our Ray-Bans. When I later made the photo my Facebook cover image, some called it our "mission from God" look, a reference to

The Blues Brothers.

Even if the media didn't portray it as such, I thought that evening was a political takedown of Baker. At times, Rick evoked an angrier side of the former mayor, who was wearing a tie with the fish symbol, an identifying symbol for Christians. On camera, in front of the audience, Baker declared that he didn't like my husband. It took eight campaigns for Rick's opponents to make it personal. Baker's pronouncement of his enmity for Rick showed a lack of humanity I hadn't seen in any of Rick's seven previous political campaigns.

It was hard to hear those words. As much as I'd hoped for some collegiality, it was now clear there would be none of that in this campaign. I resolved to spend every moment when I wasn't working or sleeping to help Rick win. That would mean uncomfortable moments answering voters' questions about baseball, the St. Pete Pier and sewage.

Chapter 16

THE ART
OF CONVERSATION

After 23 years in the same neighborhood, I still didn't know the woman I waved to every time I saw her walking her two black and white basset hound-mix dogs.

When I offered to canvass neighborhoods for Rick's reelection campaign, the first list from field director Adrienne Bogen was for our neighborhood. She thought it made sense for me to be the one to ask for their votes.

The mayor's race was nonpartisan, but this election had already pitted many Democrats against Republicans. My job was to connect with no-party affiliation (NPA) voters who didn't identify with a political party. Jordan and I arrived at the first house on the list. A man's name was on the list, but it was the woman I always waved to as she walked her dogs who answered the door.

I hadn't known where this neighbor lived, or whether she had a husband. I introduced myself and asked to speak with the man, since he was the NPA voter in the house. He popped his head out of the room where he was watching television to tell me I'd be better off speaking with his wife. He'd already decided whom he was voting for, he said.

Their dogs could smell the scent of our dogs, so they hovered around my ankles and licked my legs while I tried to recite my unrehearsed spiel.

We'd never met, but the woman knew I was the mayor's wife. I asked her whether she had decided who would get her vote in the primary.

She didn't answer my question, but she told me that Rick never waved when she walked her dogs around the lake in front of our home. I knew that wasn't true. He was always at work when she walked her dogs. But I didn't want her to dismiss us before I had a chance to persuade her to vote for Rick, so I brushed it off.

"Oh, he must be tired," I said, defending my husband for the nonexistent slight. "Maybe he was on the phone and didn't see you."

This house was our first stop, but Jordan and I were already sweating. It was 4 p.m. in August, with barely a breeze and an abundance of humidity. The neighbor motioned for us to sit down while she offered us water. We sat but declined the water. I was already uncomfortable at her combative assertion that Rick regularly snubbed her. I didn't want to linger, and I wanted to get to all the homes on the six-page list before dinnertime. It's not a good idea to interrupt someone's dinner by asking for votes.

The neighbor told me that she and her husband knew all about Rick Baker, Rick's most formidable opponent. She recited his stances on issues, his record of supporting the Rays and his opinion on a new pier. I wondered if she had me confused with Baker's wife.

"You know, my son and his friends are involved in the Republican club at the University of Tampa," she said.

I didn't know that. Until a few minutes ago, I didn't even know her name or that she had a husband or a son.

I smiled and nodded. I tried to find common ground in what I could tell was going to be a tense conversation. I told her that Jordan, who was seated next to me, had friends who attended the University of Tampa.

She didn't seem interested in what I had to say – yet.

"My son and his friends hold luncheons here each Sunday to talk about politics," she said. "They've talked about why I should vote for Rick Baker to be our next mayor."

As she talked about her son and the political luncheons, I wondered how to redirect the conversation so that I could tell her about my Rick.

Before I had the chance, she asked, "What's this problem with sewage?"

I explained that more than a year before, the antiquated sewage system failed when heavy rains overwhelmed the system. Rick had to decide whether to discharge sewage into the bay or let it flow down city streets and into homes.

She knew that Rick was fixing the system, but she wanted to know how he would prevent future discharges. When I began to answer, she reassured me she already knew what I was going to say. She was ready to move on to another subject.

"Tell me about baseball," she said.

She wanted to know how Rick would keep the Tampa Bay Rays in St. Petersburg. I told her that Rick wouldn't give up the team if he could help it, but that he also wouldn't burden taxpayers with the cost of a new stadium. Rick had been criticized in the media and by his opponents for allowing the team to look at stadium sites in other cities.

I reassured her that Rick had a good relationship with the Rays' owners and administrators. I told her our baseball team likely wasn't going anywhere.

Twenty minutes in, she brought up the Pier. Construction on the new St. Pete Pier had begun weeks earlier, and the project was a campaign topic among the mayoral candidates. Baker preferred the designs that incorporated the inverted pyramid from the old Pier. If he won, he vowed to change the design that had been selected by Rick and his administration.

Like this neighbor, voters wanted to be reassured that the costs for all the elements at the new Pier - restaurants, marketplaces, public art, green spaces, a splash pad, and a state-of-the-art accessible playground – wouldn't be passed on to them through higher taxes.

I told my neighbor that she would love the new Pier, and that it would be a place for everyone, as it should be.

I didn't mind answering her questions, even when she asked them a second, then a third time.

If my answers might have a shred of influence on her vote, and that of her friends who attended her son's political luncheons, I was willing to continue talking with her. I regretted not accepting that bottle of water, though. My mouth was parched.

I didn't need to rely on the notes provided by the campaign. Baseball, sewage and the Pier weren't just talking points. Rick cared deeply about each of these issues because they affected every resident. He cared about protecting future generations so they wouldn't have to worry about sewage spills or a baseball stadium that raised taxes. Despite opposition from many, Rick was building a new pier that would be a destination for all, not just a requisite stop when visitors come to town.

The neighbor must have been satisfied with my answers. She abruptly stood up and told me she would mail her ballot early before a month-long trip to Venezuela. She promised to learn more about Rick via his website. Her husband never came out of the room where he was watching television, not even when his wife showed Jordan and me his medals and commendations from his service in the Vietnam War.

Her dogs continued to lick my legs, as I handed her campaign literature. She told me she would remember everything I told her about sewage, baseball and the Pier. She would tell her friends, too, she said. Then, the 45-minute conversation finally ended.

Outside, I asked Jordan if she believed her. She shrugged. We hoped she would take the time to learn about both Ricks. I knew that if she did, she almost certainly would vote for my Rick. She would've never invited us into her home if her decision had already been made.

When I wasn't knocking on doors to speak to residents in neighborhoods throughout St. Pete, I was on the phone. I worked part time, so I could make calls during the mid-afternoon, then canvass for a couple of hours until dinnertime. Most nights from around 7 to 8:30, I worked my way through a list that targeted voters who hadn't returned their mail-in ballots. The campaign had provided a script and talking points, but after the first few calls, I created my own version that hit the highlights, noting Rick's platform and the deadline to return ballots. I hadn't phone banked since Rick's first campaign for the state House. During the first several calls, I prayed the voters' answering machines would pick up, so I could leave messages instead of engaging in conversations. Most of the time, the voters picked up. Only a few people hung up on me, which didn't bother me. I noted it on the call sheet and moved on to the next name.

Most people were surprised to hear that it was the mayor's wife calling. Some were grateful to have someone hear their concerns. The more calls I made, the more comfortable I became talking to people I didn't know. A necessary means to an end became an enjoyable exercise in getting to know my husband's constituents.

I talked to other St. Petersburg natives who loved telling me about the neighborhood they'd lived in their entire lives. I heard the pride in their voices. Some of them invited me for a visit to learn more, or to a Sunday church service.

Other voters told me Rick was doing a good job, which was humbling. The best words I heard were that a voter, or sometimes their entire household, had already returned their ballots and voted for Rick. I put a big star next to their names, so the field team could update the database.

This was the first time in Rick's almost 18 years in politics that voters asked about me. Some of them wanted to know what I did for a job, how old our kids were, and how long I'd lived in St. Pete. When I told them that I was born at St. Anthony's Hospital near downtown, they couldn't believe they were talking to a St. Pete native. We're rare. Many St. Pete residents are transplants from the North or Midwest.

With every call, I took a deep breath. Sometimes, a voter apologetically told me they were going to vote for someone else. I thanked them for taking my call and for participating in the democratic process. Most names on the phone lists were strangers, but we shared the same love for St. Pete. My conversations with them told me they cared who their leaders were.

I made notes in the margins when voters had questions for Rick. I relayed their concerns to him in a synopsis email each evening. I looked forward to the next day, when I returned to campaign headquarters to turn in my phone list to volunteers who entered the data. I left with a new list that I started on each night after dinner.

On Mondays, I drove Jordan and three classmates to north Tampa for Irish step dancing classes. Between the drive, classes and stopping for dinner afterward, it was a six-hour round trip. Instead of running errands or chatting with other dance parents, I sat in the parking lot in my car and called voters. The cliché of every vote counting would be true in this election. We were worried that Rick might not make it through the Aug. 24 primary. Polls pointed to the possibility that Rick could lose in the primary.

The night of the primary election, the mood was somber as we waited upstairs at the State Theater. We could hear the crowd below, but we couldn't decipher whether the talking or occasional cheering was a good sign. My heart pounded every time campaign manager Jacob Smith hit refresh on the supervisor of elections website.

My nervous stomach wouldn't let me eat until I knew whether Rick would continue to the general election. It churned with a combination of nausea and excitement until we heard the screaming downstairs. Rick had not only survived the primary, but he finished first with 48.36 percent of the vote – a margin of just 70 votes. He and Baker, who got 48.23 percent, would move to a runoff on Nov. 7.

Rick may have squeaked through the primary, but that night the campaign's trajectory changed. Voters, pollsters and even *Tampa Bay Times* political editor Adam C. Smith expected Baker to earn enough votes in the primary to win the race. When he didn't, the former mayor launched into an angry on-camera tirade, a side of him that many St. Pete voters had never seen.

I was relieved to have the opportunity to spend more afternoons, evenings and weekends canvassing and calling. I looked forward to meeting more constituents. Imagine my surprise when one of them was a real-life mermaid.

— Chapter 17 —

A MERMAID, A BIDEN, AND A BEARD

When she was a preschooler, Jordan's favorite Disney princess was Belle, the beauty who captivates the beast, not Ariel the mermaid, the preferred princess of her peers.

We never read the "The Little Mermaid," the classic Hans Christian Andersen tale, nor did we watch the movie, which chronicled Ariel's desire to trade her life as a sea creature for a human soul.

Ariel's goal was love. Lately, mine had been, too. I hoped that the voters I spoke with would love Rick enough to elect him to a second term. When I telephoned a 94-year-old voter on my campaign call list, I had no idea she would be the inspiration I needed to keep pushing to election day.

Canvassing Neighborhoods - 2017

Less than two weeks after Rick won the primary, campaigning came to a temporary halt. Hurricane Irma, a Category 4 storm, was headed toward Tampa Bay. I packed a portable mattress, towels and bedding for Rick for his three-day stay at the emergency operations center. Jordan came home from Gainesville. I picked up Wilder, a guide dog in training at the Southeastern Guide Dogs campus, which was being evacuated. Deputy Mayor Kanika Tomalin's golden retriever Petey moved in, and my 84-year-old stepmother-in-law arrived with her overnight bag and a bottle of vodka.

I took pictures off the walls and photographed our possessions in case the insurance company needed proof of our losses. Our walk-in closet was the only windowless space large enough for the kids, my mother-in-law, four dogs and me. That was where we would hunker down, if necessary, when the storm came through.

Fortunately, the storm weakened, and its path shifted eastward in the final hours. Many St. Petersburg residents lost power for days, but the city was spared the catastrophic damage many had feared. Rick's leadership during that tense time got positive coverage in the news media and praise from many voters.

That helped soften the blows that were coming from an unexpected source – the children of some Rick Baker supporters. Samuel was a freshman at St. Petersburg High School, and some of the students there were not welcoming.

They taunted him by telling him their parents had voted for Baker, and one of them was particularly cruel.

"Why don't you tell your dad to stop being a little bitch," he said to Samuel at their lockers between classes.

Another student superimposed Samuel's face in the middle of a Googled photo of "dead Jewish bodies" and sent the image to other students via Snapchat. The police interviewed Samuel at our home. What the student did amounted to a hate crime, but Samuel, Rick and I were satisfied that the student only received a suspension. We didn't want to cause any further anguish to Samuel. If the student had been arrested and charged with a crime against the mayor's son, it surely would have made the news.

On a rare Sunday when Rick had a few hours free from campaigning, he took Samuel to the golf course. A group of boys teased them by doing donuts in a golf cart while yelling, "We love Rick Baker." The damage to the course, not their words, got the boys permanently banned.

Hate is exhausting. It would've been easy to retreat. If it wasn't for a 94-year-old woman's sweet demeanor and heartfelt words, I might've never made another campaign call. I had barely finished introducing myself when she cut to the chase. She would vote for Rick. I started to thank her, but she continued...

"Do you know I am an original Weeki Wachee mermaid?"

Locals and tourists have visited Weeki Wachee State Park, one of Florida's oldest attractions, since it opened in 1947. It's known for its mermaids, the young women who perform synchronized dance moves under water in the Mermaid Theater while breathing through air hoses hidden in the scenery.

Unlike mermaid folklore that preaches doom and gloom, my conversation with this real-life mermaid plucked me out of the dread I felt about the campaign. She was well-versed on Rick's political history. She remembered his 2001 swing vote on the City Council when the Southwest Florida Water Management District (SWFWMD) wanted to buy Weeki Wachee. Rick ended up being the deciding vote – and his vote was no to the sale. He wanted a covenant that would forever protect the land. Immediately after the vote, Mayor Baker told Rick that if he would ask for the matter to be reconsidered, SWFWMD would provide the requested covenant. Rick moved to reconsider, and with his yes vote the deal passed. More importantly, it preserved the state park as a natural resource.

The former mermaid renewed my belief that the campaign was on the right track, just the jolt I needed before I was unexpectedly interviewed a few days later after Rick and I cast our early votes.

When *Tampa Bay Times* reporter Divya Kumar asked my opinion about the campaign, I told her it had been a wonderful experience. Even though it was the nastiest of Rick's eight campaigns, I relished my positive conversations with voters. I told her I was excited about the campaign, which would continue to move the city forward. After the story was published, campaign manager Jacob Smith and media consultant John Rowley texted me their approval.

Election day began with early morning sign waving at a busy intersection. I conducted my own straw poll by gauging the number of honks and thumbs-up versus thumbs-down and other gestures. I tried not to get my hopes up. It would be a long day. On my drive to Gainesville to pick up Jordan at the University of Florida, Rick updated me with reports of positive conversations with voters on the phone and at the polls.

Later that afternoon, as I procrastinated getting ready for the election night party, I told Rick we would be okay if he didn't win. Such cliché words, as I knew he would be devastated if he lost what he called the best job he ever had. I couldn't let myself believe the recent polls that showed him a few points ahead.

Our security officer, Dennis, picked us up at 6 p.m. to take us to NOVA 535. Rick and I could barely respond to his polite conversation. I felt like I was on my way to a funeral. I was nauseous, and my mouth felt like sandpaper.

Each time a precinct reported votes, Rick's lead grew. The mood intensified. Rick rocked back and forth, hands on his knees, head between his legs. He took deep breaths while I rubbed his back. I glanced over at Jordan and Samuel, who were sitting in a plush corner sofa with Kai and Nia Tomalin, the children of Deputy Mayor Kanika Tomalin. They'd never seen their father like this, not even when our house burned or when he was hospitalized for an immune disorder.

I needed to focus on Rick, but I felt like I was going to vomit. Someone got me water. No one said a word, as the margin between Rick and Baker kept growing. Champagne was uncorked, and glasses were distributed. The room buzzed with phones and chatter. People started hugging.

Omar Kahn, a friend who had worked in the Obama administration, told Rick he needed to find his phone so he could take a call.

Before the primary, former President Obama had publicly endorsed Rick. It was only the second time the former president weighed in on a city election. Darryl Paulson, professor emeritus of government at The University of South Florida St. Petersburg, described it as an unusual move. Days before the general election, former Vice President Joe Biden recorded a robocall for Rick.

It was Biden who was calling to congratulate Rick on his win. Rick held the phone so the kids and I could hear. I snapped a photo with my cell phone to forever commemorate the moment.

It felt good to win, but the immediate celebration was marred. The 2013 campaign ended with a gracious concession by Bill Foster. We waited for a concession call from Baker before greeting the crowd. He never called.

Election Night - 2017

The kids and I stood by as Rick thanked voters for giving him a second term. He has never given me flowers for my birthday, Valentine's Day or our anniversary. It's too obvious, he says. That night, I choked back tears while holding a huge bouquet of flowers from Rick.

There was no after party in a presidential suite this time. After a late-night dinner of Joey Brooklyn's pizza, we joined the team at Blue Goose for cocktails, pool and video games.

The next morning, Rick gave phone interviews while he drove Jordan back to Gainesville. It was a new chapter, a second term. By now, we were used to what felt like non-stop media coverage, but soon there would be a more personal story to cover, about the choice Rick made the day after the election to stop shaving.

What's with the beard, many wanted to know. No one noticed the winter goatee or beard Rick sported each winter. Now, people wondered if his new look was part of "No Shave November" or an effort to disguise himself after the election. I joked about creating an Instagram profile just for "the beard."

People asked me if I liked the beard. They wanted to know why he grew it and how long it would last. I couldn't tell them. I was used to answering questions about Rick's politics, but questions about his facial hair left me at a loss for words.

I have spent many hours over the last 20 years in the hairdresser's chair with foil coming out of my head so I could have blonde highlights in my dark brown hair. Lately, I'd returned to my natural color. No one asked Rick what he thought of my hair.

Most men refrain from commenting on women's hair or wardrobe. Everyone thought it was fair game to question Rick's beard. I didn't get it, but I was grateful that people were talking about something besides the campaign.

Politicians usually avoid growing facial hair. Something about trust or a certain connotation a beard implies. In a 2015 *GQ* article, Oklahoma State University professor Rebekah Herrick conducted a study that determined that fewer than 5% of congressmen have facial hair. The reason? They don't want to appear insensitive to women's issues. According to Herrick, women subconsciously perceived politicians with beards and mustaches as being less feminist, regardless of their voting records.

Not in Rick's case. Other women complimented him, and I agreed with them when they told me how handsome he looked. Many thought he looked younger. The beard was here to stay, so I stocked up on beard oil, conditioner and grooming products for Rick for birthdays and holidays.

I was used to answering questions about almost everything that related to Rick's political career. Now, I talked about his beard. When *Tampa Bay Times* reporter Zack Sampson wrote a story about the beard, I was surprised I wasn't interviewed.

"I've been quite honestly shocked by the attention this beard has received," Rick told Sampson. "It seems to have a life of its own."

Sampson asked if the beard was an appeal to millennials, many of whom have beards, or whether it was for "No Shave November." It was none of that, and no one saw it as a bad omen. People pay attention more than we realize, and sometimes they make assumptions about who we are without knowing us.

In post-election conversations with other civic leaders and acquaintances, people started to ask me how I survive political life. Until the 2017 race, all the questions were for Rick. Their interest in my experience as a political spouse showed me that many viewed politics as a partnership. Many in the city were emotionally invested in this race. They understood what it was like to advocate for the candidate of your choice, as well as what it feels like to almost lose. I enjoyed talking about my experiences in the political spotlight. I appreciated the recognition of the role I played in Rick's success. That's not why I made thousands of calls, stood on doorsteps and endured grilling in a constituent's living room. I believed Rick was the best person for the job of mayor.

People may have had opinions about Rick's beard, but I soon discovered that some also had opinions – and monikers – for me.

Swearing In with the Hon. Mark Shames, St. Petersburg City Hall – 2018,
Tampa Bay Times, photographer Scott Keeler

— Chapter 18 —

BUILDING MY BRAND

Several months after Rick was reelected mayor, we attended the unveiling of a piece of public art. While the event's co-host talked with Rick, his business partner chatted me up.

"So how do you do this?" he asked, then quickly answered his own question.

"You're really just arm candy, aren't you?"

Bam! Those seven undiplomatic words reflect the kind of comments that I'll bet just about every female political spouse hears. Over the years, I have been called everything from arm candy and Stepford wife (you know, servile and submissive, catering to my husband's every whim) to Rick's secret weapon.

The man who wanted to affix the arm candy label on me got an earful about my longevity as a city resident, my family, my volunteer work and my job as the public relations manager for a nonprofit that serves people with disabilities. I'm certain he got the message. But others also have been quick to define me.

My life as the spouse of a public figure has evolved with every campaign and office that Rick has held. Our lives have changed in good ways and bad. Winning is wonderful, but then life changes almost overnight.

When Rick was elected mayor, I expected his profile to be elevated, not mine. But because I was now first lady of St. Pete, people were suddenly interested in me. I was invited to present awards, speak about civic engagement, and sit and be photographed for interviews in local magazines.

I wasn't prepared for the attention.

Most political spouses do not have the benefit of a team that crafts an identity, communicates a consistent message, and provides talking points when needed. We enter the political world as enthusiastic supporters and loyal comrades. Sometimes, we shun the spotlight and choose indifference. We're either all in, or we remain on the periphery. We balance being a political spouse with nurturing our own goals and interests. Some see us as a nicely dressed package of sound bites and clichés. Others see us as an equal partner in the political package.

"How do you do this?" is the number one question I'm asked. Rarely am I asked if I have a job. People know all about Rick, but they don't know me. A front-row seat to politics is a study in human perception. I've been placed in certain categories based on others' assumptions of who they think I am.

I'm often surprised by how others see me. "Arm candy" made me feel diminished. "Stepford wife" conjured memories of the 1975 movie based on the novel that chronicled a town full of too-perfect women. I never imagined that anyone would consider me such an integral part of Rick's campaign that I would be anointed his secret weapon.

Words carry weight. I try to choose mine carefully, whether spoken or written online.

More than six months after Rick was reelected for a second term, people still talked about the 2017 mayor's race. More people than ever asked me how I tolerated the political spotlight.

Rick's eighth political campaign was the most contentious the city had seen in decades. Even though Rick won, I was skeptical of anyone who purported to support him afterward. I wanted to protect him from those who sought his attention again after not supporting his reelection.

The rose-colored lenses through which I'd viewed the political world early on were muddied. I was armed with a new elevator speech that focuses on survival, since that's what so many of the people I spoke with after the 2017 campaign seemed to be interested in.

When the man who made the arm candy comment wrongfully assumed I was nothing more than what Merriam-Webster defines as a "young attractive person who accompanies a usually older person to social events," I buried the label and changed the conversation's trajectory.

Political spouses must be the authors of their own stories. We determine *who* we are, and *how* we show ourselves to the world. When people want to know how I survive the public scrutiny, disrupted schedules and the 24/7 life of a mayor, I let them in.

Years of practice have trained me to prepare, respond and deflect diminishing comments while barely taking a breath. Instead of being delicate like a grain of sand, I try to be the strong pearl Jimmy Buffett sings about in "Oysters and Pearls."

Like the grain of sand that through disruption and transformation becomes a pearl, I'm an unfinished project. But I'm the only artist of my story. My journey from sand to pearl is different than another's. It was up to me to control the narrative about how others perceive me. I disrupted the norms and stereotypes many have about political spouses, especially women.

It's fair to say that most people who had a Facebook account, voter I.D. and St. Pete ZIP code were engaged in the 2017 mayor's race. Factions formed among business sectors, in social cliques and neighborhood communities. Alliances were formed, then destroyed. Friends became enemies.

Many people reached out to me with information they thought might help the campaign. Monsignor Robert Gibbons, the leader at my childhood parish, St. Paul's, occasionally messaged me with suggestions for Rick.

He shared what he heard from chatter at the church, barber shop and popular breakfast spots. A barber shop owner who was a parish member told Monsignor that he only had signs for Baker. As a business owner, he wanted to allow all candidates to place signs in his shop. He wanted to appear neutral, but he told Monsignor he would vote for Rick. Monsignor politely but urgently suggested I ask campaign staffers to deliver signs to the shop. Pronto.

I didn't mind being Monsignor's direct link to Rick. I enjoyed a rapport that's not possible when you're a student wearing a plaid skirt, white Peter Pan-collared shirt, and knee socks. Back then, priests and nuns were authority figures, not allies.

After Rick was reelected, he and Monsignor met for lunch. They dissected the campaign and spoke of St. Pete's future. Monsignor called me Rick's secret weapon. Whether true or not, that moniker is much better than arm candy or Stepford wife.

I've always supported Rick's political aspirations and helped on campaigns where I could, but I never elevated myself to that role. Some political spouses demand positions on the campaign team.

I steadfastly served alongside staffers and volunteers. If asked, I appeared in television ads, recorded robocalls, and served as a surrogate for Rick. When I had an opinion about something related to the campaign, I told Rick first. If he felt it warranted a mention to the campaign team, he shared it.

Perhaps Monsignor recognized that my behind-the-scenes support was an asset because it allowed the team to do its job without distraction. In private, Rick and I prayed, strategized, and vented often during that 2017 race. I sensed Monsignor knew our struggles.

Before that election, I hadn't considered the power of political spouses to be influencers. I never considered myself a secret weapon, but I knew that how political spouses show themselves to the world can be the difference between winning and losing.

Unless you're the spouse of a high-level politician and have your own staff, political spouses are their own brand ambassadors. Time served as a veteran political spouse doesn't render one immune from the stereotypes. There will always be an architect who thinks you're "arm candy," or a backhanded compliment that says you're nothing more than a well-dressed robot. Then your parish priest calls you a "secret weapon."

I've been a working professional, a stay-at-home-mom, a community volunteer, an entrepreneur. I've learned to hone my role as political spouse. I try to go through life with confidence, candor and poise while advocating and promoting my own brand. I've grown from an uneasy, naive political spouse into one who is confident and comfortable in her role.

Sometimes I forget that people are paying attention. Rick might be the public figure in the relationship. But every so often, I'm reminded that people are watching what I do and what I say, even when I'm hundreds of miles away from St. Pete in the middle of the ocean.

— Chapter 19 —

WATCHING MY WORDS

Since my first college fraternity party in 1986, when it was confirmed that rum and I would never get along, I avoided even sniffing Rick's favorites, Papa's Pilar and Zaya. I hadn't touched the stuff for almost 30 years until I sat at the table with our travel companions at a private restaurant on the second floor of a home in Havana. We were there for the 2016 exhibition baseball game between the Rays and the Cuban national team. The mojito that took 20 minutes to craft was as beautiful as the surrounding vistas and view of Morro Castle, the centuries-old colonial fortress. Best of all, I didn't get sick.

Three years later, we were headed back to Havana on a cruise with 15 family members and friends to celebrate the 75th birthdays of my mom and stepfather Fred.

Rick was a three-time traveler to Havana, so he created the itinerary which, after a stop in Key West, had us visiting Revolutionary Square, sipping daquiris at El Floridita, and strolling the Malecon, the shoreline walkway where the locals gather. Pastel-colored vintage 1950s cars would take us to the open-air art market and to Hotel Nacional for Hemingway's favorite cocktail, the mojito.

We opted out of booking shore excursions through the cruise line. That meant we had to wait for most of the passengers to disembark before we could leave the ship to explore Key West.

For more than an hour, we sat on the carpeted steps near the exit. I passed the time scrolling through Facebook vacation photos, recycled news, sad images of foster dogs, and political debates.

While we waited to hear, "Group 11 may now disembark the ship," I saw a headline that made me wish I were already sipping a margarita at Captain Tony's Saloon.

"Trump Admin Imposes New Restrictions on Travel to Cuba."

CNN and other news outlets reported that educational peo-ple-to-people type of travel to Cuba would be restricted after June 5, 2019. I scanned the story to see what impact it would have on cruise ship travelers. The story implied that reservations made before June 5 would stand. It was June 4. Our ship was scheduled to dock in Havana on June 5. I looked for more stories on the ban while I reassured everyone that we were still going to Havana.

My frustration over our dwindling time in Key West grew as we waited our turn to disembark.

I was getting antsy. Even though I try to keep my Facebook page positive and free from politically charged posts, I wrote:

"This doesn't solve problems some perceive that the U.S. has with Cuba. Glad we're getting in under the wire as our ship arrives in Havana tomorrow, June 5." I pasted the link to the CNN story, then hit "share."

Thirty minutes later, I heard, "Group 11 may now disembark the ship." I shut off my phone and headed with our group to the trolley that would deposit us at a touristy shopping village. Over five hours, we visited Ernest Hemingway's home, ate lunch at Sloppy Joe's, and shopped for hats. We finished with a trolley tour that didn't even stop at the colorful concrete buoy that Key West marketers say is the southernmost point of the continental United States, where we'd hoped to snap a group photo. By 6, we were back on the ship to shower and dress for dinner.

Shortly before 8, Rick and I headed to the stern to see the sunset before joining the others for dinner. Gasps and expletives inter-rupted our sunset selfies. The whipping wind and rumbling en-gines muffled the words, but when we heard "the president" and "diverting to Nassau" broadcast through the speakers, we knew we weren't going to Havana.

The next morning, Rick and I thanked our lucky stars that our ship wasn't already in Cuba with other stalled ships. We perched at the ship's bow to take in the view on our approach to Nassau. Rows of palm trees flanked the gargantuan Atlantis Resort. The pastel-colored buildings reflected in the azure Atlantic Ocean was a lovely site, but it wasn't Havana.

We'd traded Havana's mojitos for Senor Frog's dive bar. While we toured the markets and dodged vendors who wanted to sell us everything straw that said Nassau, I got a notification on my phone. We had Wi-Fi, so I checked social media.

The first notification was a friend request from *Tampa Bay Times* reporter Josh Solomon, who covers City Hall. Then I saw a WhatsApp message from Kevin King, Rick's chief of policy and public engagement.

"Do you or Rick have cell service?" he asked.

"I don't think so," I said. "All ok? We are in Nassau."

"Media calling us," he said. "We did a statement."

"About what?" I asked. "Cuba?"

"Yes," he said.

Apparently, when a political decision by the president affects a mayor's vacation it's news. Even though we wouldn't make it to Havana, we were still enjoying ourselves. I thought about the families I saw on our ship with dozens of suitcases and boxed big screen televisions that were obviously for family members they'd planned to see in Cuba. I wondered whether reporters would want to know how they felt when they learned they wouldn't see their families in Cuba.

Everyone has stories to tell of vacation plans gone awry. We'd add this to the list of the train crash I was in when I was a teen and the time Rick tore his ACL on the first day of our ski trip, which had already been delayed two days due to fog. While disappointing, this inconvenience didn't seem like news to me. The *Times,* and television and radio stations back home, disagreed.

The mayor's family had been directly affected by President Trump's sudden decision to halt Americans' travel to Cuba. That decision halted the progress that had been made toward restored relations between the U.S. and Cuba. Rick had been outspoken since December 2015, when Trump – then a presidential candidate — tweeted his suggestion that Muslims should be banned from entering the United States.

My hastily written post created a news cycle that required Rick's staff to craft a statement and field reporters' phone calls about something his staff knew nothing about. It was the first time that my words impacted Rick's job.

Rick reframed my guilt over the post as an opportunity to respond to the president's punitive decision, which inconvenienced thousands of cruise ship passengers and threatened to destroy inroads the U.S. had made toward restored relations with Cuba. The

Cuban economy had surged after President Obama lifted sanctions in April 2015. Americans traveled to Cuba. American businesses invested in Cuba. New hotels opened. Wi-Fi was installed. Infrastructure was beginning to be restored. With the stroke of his pen, Trump stopped progress.

When we returned to Port Canaveral, Rick's phone buzzed with reporters' requests to film our family as we disembarked the ship. We advised the rest of our group to walk separately from us if they didn't want to be interviewed or filmed.

My Facebook post may have caught the attention of local media, but the image of news trucks and Spanish television stations waiting to interview Rick and other cruise ship passengers signaled that the travel ban carried significant implications. It was an international story.

That evening, after we returned to St. Pete, Rick went to City Hall for more interviews about our trip and what Trump's new policy meant for future relations with Cuba. If it hadn't been for my 28-word Facebook post, our trip might never have been news. It reminded me that someone is always watching.

Since social media became a prevalent tool to communicate, I've grappled countless times with whether to use my voice to speak out or stay neutral. My name has never been on a ballot, but I'm the closest person to Rick, who *is* elected.

Whether I like it or not, being first lady gives me a platform. I'm cognizant that my actions and words can reflect positively or negatively on Rick. Tweets live in perpetuity, so I try to be careful with mine. I usually resist rather than engage with those who seek to disparage Rick. I walk a tightrope between citizen and political spouse. With a carefully crafted message, I can be both without affecting Rick's ability to do his job.

When someone on Twitter replied to a photo of Pinellas County Commissioner Ken Welch and Rick at a fundraiser for a domestic violence shelter with, "When will you stop beating your wife?" I responded swiftly. I told the person their comment was a lie and that their accusation about my husband did a disservice to the organization's mission to eradicate domestic violence.

Rick was the city's first mayor to use social media to inform and engage with the community. I often saw the negative comments, but I usually refused to engage with the cowards who would never say in public what they wrote online. Sometimes, I crafted responses that were never posted, which helped me cycle through the emotions of seeing hateful words written about Rick.

Some words are truly better left unsaid, and unwritten.

When St. Pete Beach Commissioner Melinda Pletcher grew angry in 2019 about a proposal for bus rapid transit between St. Pete and St. Pete Beach, she called Rick's argument for the plan a "Mafia move." The Mob is no longer active in the Tampa Bay area, but as an Italian, it felt like a dog whistle to me.

While the comment percolated in my mind. I composed a possible response that I shared with Rick.

"I'd really love to post this," I said.

I never did post the 140 words about how her comment offended someone of Italian heritage who has heard a lot of ethnic jokes and slurs. An offhand comment from a disgruntled commissioner that many didn't seem to notice wasn't worth potentially starting an online argument.

My skin may be thick, but I will always protect and defend those I love. When I do, it's because someone made it personal.

Leading up to Rick's final year as mayor, some St. Pete City Council members sought to limit his authority as mayor. In a series of political maneuvers, they tried to strip Rick of the executive powers he enjoyed in St. Petersburg's strong-mayor form of government. Some council members were argumentative, even petty.

When a photo circulated on social media of Rick at the Tampa Bay Rays' 2021 home opener without a mask, many scolded him online. The photo was shot from behind, and it didn't show the beer and pretzel he was eating, which was the only time patrons were permitted to remove their masks. At the next City Council meeting, council member Robert Blackmon introduced a measure to strip Rick of emergency executive powers. In his presentation, Blackmon called Rick's Covid-safe policies a dictatorship and cited the photo from the game as an example of Rick's hypocrisy over mask wearing. Blackmon neglected to mention he also was photographed without a mask at the same game.

The council member's comments had veered from policy to personal. He'd gone too far. I tweeted my defense of Rick's aggressive Covid-safe policies as leadership, not a dictatorship.

Two days later, a *Times* story by Solomon detailed Rick's increasingly rocky relationship with the City Council. A photo of my two tweets capped off the story.

Solomon didn't interview me, but he correctly surmised that my tweets were about Blackmon's comments. One half of a political couple in the news is enough, but when a news story mentions both of us, I'm reminded of my personal checklist for commenting, posting and tweeting:

Will this matter tomorrow, next year, or in five years?

Am I responding to a real person or a bot?

Does my message advocate for a cause important to me, or an issue that affects many?

Is it worth a few minutes of satisfaction if a message shared hurts a political campaign or causes unnecessary interference with my or Rick's job?

Writing letters that never get sent or responses that are never posted helps me sort through feelings of anger and frustration. I reply and post from a place of advocacy for others, myself or my family.

In December 2019, a different kind of social media post became necessary. On a family trip to Pebble Beach, California, to watch Samuel play with pro golfers, I wound up in the hospital – the first event in a year that would test my faith. Suddenly, I needed to publicly disclose that I had cancer.

— Chapter 20 —

SEVEN MONTHS TO LIVE

The doctor was so casual she might as well have been recounting what she ate for lunch. The words that rolled off her tongue took my breath away. The bloating, fevers and chills I'd experienced for three weeks now had a cause.

"You have a 20-centimeter tumor on your right ovary," she said.

The words replayed like an incessant ringing in my ears.

I trust it's not easy to tell someone they likely have cancer, but her words were a punch in the gut. In the age of social media and ugly politics, I've been exposed to plenty of shocking words. Yet, none of those words shook me like this.

No one knows how to respond when they're told they have a tumor three times the height of a golf tee, half as tall as a bowling pin, and one-tenth the height of Shaquille O'Neal. I thought I had a virus. It turned out to be a life-threatening disease.

That's probably why the emergency room doctor's notes described me as "an incredibly pleasant 51-year-old... and... appropriately shocked and in disbelief."

"Oh no, are you sure?" was my first response. She was right. I was in disbelief.

Minutes later, a nurse whisked me away to another room one floor above. As I lay on my left side, a doctor probed my abdomen with a fearsome looking needle to extract more than two cups of yellow, turbid fluid.

The doctor also had a 16-year-old, a daughter. He asked why I was in California. As he inserted a narrower needle so that he could dig deeper, I told him about Samuel's golf tournament in two days at Pebble Beach.

A few minutes later, the on-call hospital gynecologist appeared. The dark room couldn't hide the pain and fear or soften her patronizing words.

"I just left your amazingly handsome husband," she said. That was code for, "I don't really have anything good to tell you, so I'll distract you with compliments."

She told me she was sorry. I asked her if the size of the tumor meant it was malignant. She said a test showed that the amount of the protein CA 125 in my blood — called a "CA 125 tumor marker" — was 931. Normal is 35 or lower.

I was desperate for a smidgen of positive news, but all this insensitive gynecologist did was ask how many kids I had, how old they were, how many live births I'd had, and whether I'd ever taken oral contraceptives. There *might* be options to prolong my life, she said, as she gave me the "there have been many advancements in treatment" speech.

Without knowing what a battery of pathology tests might show, she told me the cancer had likely spread and could be stage 4. I was still appropriately shocked and in disbelief, but all I heard was "7-8 months."

I refused to believe I would die within the year.

Hours later, I was admitted to a private room. While I fumbled with the hospital gown that wouldn't tie properly, my feet perspired in the mandatory non-skid socks. "FALL RISK" was printed on the white board.

No one heard me say "fuck this shit" to Rick as I fiddled with the tubes from my I.V. fluids and antibiotics.

"Tumor my ass," I said.

Not the most appropriate language for a first lady, but what do you say when a doctor who has none of your prior medical history, no pathology reports, and only a CT scan and blood work results says you could die in seven or eight months?

"I'm not ready to die," I told Rick.

I kept asking him, "Do I look like someone who is going to die?' He patiently and affirmatively answered, "No, you aren't going to die," and, "No, you don't look sick."

This was not what I envisioned when Samuel learned he was one of 78 junior golfers selected to play in the Pure Insurance Championship tournament. The tournament benefits the First Tee, a nonprofit youth development organization that sponsors golf programs designed to build character. Samuel dreamed of playing in this tournament since he was 5, but his handicap of two didn't guarantee automatic entry. He thoughtfully composed responses to six essay prompts, volunteered 100 hours helping younger golfers at our local First Tee, answered interview questions, and completed a college entry-length application.

We were in one of the most beautiful spots in the country, and by the second day of our week-long trip, I was in the hospital, unsure of whether I'd get to see Samuel play. I'd looked forward to visiting with my cousin Quinn and her husband and kids, who lived nearby in Carmel. My aunt came from New Jersey. Jordan, who managed to mostly avoid Friday classes throughout college, came for the weekend. Rounding out our group was my mom. None of them knew the real reason for my hospitalization. I told everyone I had some gastrointestinal infection that I would deal with when we returned to St. Pete.

The truth was that I already had an appointment the next week in St. Pete with the same gynecological oncologist that treated my mom for uterine cancer five years earlier. I just wanted to feel well enough to be on the golf course when Samuel teed off at 7:48 a.m., less than 48 hours away.

On the first day of the tournament, I made sure I was showered, dressed and packed by 6 a.m. I still had a temperature of 99, which meant the attending physician might've kept me in the hospital. A nurse was kind enough to put a cold washcloth on my forehead so my temperature would read 98.6. Quinn picked me up and drove me to Pebble Beach in time to see Samuel and his professional golf partner, Greg Kraft, midway through the round.

Kraft asked where I'd been for the first nine holes. I'm sure he wondered why the mom wasn't there to see her son tee off at Pebble Beach.

"I had some business to take care of," I said.

Samuel and Greg ended the day in first place, and Samuel gave me his golf ball, which I carried in my purse for more than a year.

We told everyone in the family I had an infection and would follow up with a doctor when we returned to St. Pete. I tried to project the picture of health as I walked the hilly course. I pretended to enjoy the meals and red wine, while I hid the cold sweats and my distended belly.

Life already looked different. Now, I was likely a cancer patient, like the people for whom I'd made meals, delivered comfort baskets, and donated to Go Fund Me accounts. I'd been thrust to the other side.

After we returned to St. Pete, I apologized to my mom for lying about the infection. The next day she joined Rick and me at the gynecological oncologists's office. She and Connie, the head oncology nurse, embraced when we arrived. Connie hugged me, too. She smiled as she spoke.

I hoped that no one in the waiting room recognized Rick. Six years into an eight-year tenure as mayor of the fifth largest city in Florida, people often know his voice before they see his face. I was grateful he was there, but I wished he were invisible. If someone saw the mayor and his wife in an oncologist's office, they might tell others. I worried that the press would find out and question whether my illness might affect Rick's performance.

Connie got us into an examination room quickly, reducing the likelihood anyone would recognize us.

"We're going to get you all better," she said.

"Did you go to California like this?" the doctor asked. I felt embarrassed, as if I should have known I had a tumor before I boarded the plane.

"Did you just think you were gaining weight?" he asked.

I'd neglected my stomach crunches, but I knew my increased girth wasn't fat. I blamed my evening glass of wine and an appetite for salty snacks. I thought the extra 10 pounds was part of aging.

Within 30 minutes, I was scheduled for surgery. Eight days later, over three-and-a-half hours, my doctor removed my ovaries, uterus, omentum, and 13 lymph nodes. While I recovered, I began to share my diagnosis with people outside our family. Every time I told someone, I had to relive being hospitalized in California and hearing, "You have cancer."

My doctor told Rick and me that he removed all traces of cancer, but I chose to follow the standard treatment protocol for stage 2 ovarian and uterine cancer. I looked forward to chemotherapy and radiation. The sooner I could put this behind me, the sooner I could return to life before cancer. It was difficult to see the reactions from friends and family who worried about me, or who were cancer survivors and knew what was coming next.

My job was to stay focused and positive and draw on my faith in God.

Rick wanted to accompany me to each chemotherapy treatment, which meant that he would be out of the office one day a month for six months. Other than vacations and occasional sick days, he never took a day off. Rick's professional calendar is public record. On the date of my first chemotherapy treatment, the calendar entry read, "Mayor out."

When *Tampa Bay Times* reporter Josh Solomon questioned Rick's absence, Rick's communications director replied, "Family business."

Two days after that first chemo, we were in Orlando for another golf tournament. Over breakfast, Rick broached the subject of crafting a public statement about my diagnosis. Reporters might accept "family business" as a reason for Rick's absence once, but not five more times.

I was angry. While I was trying to heal, stay positive and reduce my stress, I had to decide whether to disclose my private health information to the world.

I knew that a statement would be necessary if we wanted to quash reporters' questions. I told Rick that I should be the one to tell the story of my stage 2 ovarian and uterine cancer, not his staff or a speculative reporter. My statement would not be a public relations event. I would give no interviews, where I might be misquoted. The media could use the information in my statement after it was posted to my Facebook page.

I opted not to mention that I had ovarian cancer, which is usually discovered in the later stages and has a grim prognosis. I didn't want people to think the mayor's wife might die. I wanted to stress that I was lucky that my cancer was caught early and that it was likely curable.

If I was going to reveal something so personal, I wanted it to inspire others who might be facing the same, or worse, challenges.

As a political spouse, and now a cancer patient, I've learned that what you say is as important as how you say it. Written or spoken, tone can be extracted, and meaning inferred. I learned from doctors who were cavalier with words just how much a bad situation can be made worse. I also learned that when delivered with care and compassion, words have the power to bring light in a very dark time.

This was my message:

There is nothing like having the support of family and friends, as I embark on a new chapter of life...

It has been said that political campaigns are like marathons. They are long, with slow starts that quickly ramp up, requiring candidates to endure long days that sap their energy and threaten to deplete their resources. Whether campaigns last 3 months or longer than a year, no one will deny that reservoirs of energy, passion, persistence, tenacity, and faith must be tapped and replenished regularly, as one would when running a marathon.

I have supported Rick through 8 political campaigns. He was the candidate, but I have endured the marathons right by his side, as his wife, friend, and advisor.

Now it is my turn to run my own type of marathon, and his turn to be by my side.

In September, we traveled to California to accompany Samuel to the biggest competition of his golf career, The Pure Insurance Championship Benefitting the First Tee. Mild discomfort that began earlier that month came to a head on our second day in Monterey. A visit to the emergency room, along with a series of tests and scans revealed an infection that required me to be given I.V. antibiotics and hospitalized for two days. Thankfully, I responded to the antibiotic in time to be released the morning of the first day of the tournament. I was able to make it to the course, just as Samuel finished the first 9 holes on the Pebble Beach Golf Course. He gave me his ball from that day, which he finished tied for first place. I carry it with me every day.

But that was not all those scans and tests revealed.

They also revealed cancer.

Rick and I held onto our secret from those tests that week, as this was an important week for Samuel, and we were visiting family who lived in Carmel, and had my mom, Jordan, and aunt with us, too.

The week of our return to St. Pete, I met with a doctor who, after reviewing my medical records from California, scheduled surgery the following week. The surgery was successful, and I am grateful for a good prognosis, that the cancer was caught early.

We still do not know the source of the infection, but by the grace of God, it alerted physicians to what was going on inside of me. Had I not become ill in California my prognosis could have been much different.

Cancer has a way of providing clarity. The gratefulness I thought I felt daily and overall, prior to my diagnosis pales in comparison to how I feel now. Cancer challenges you to confront fears, and it tests your faith. It brings amazing gifts from people all around you. I do not believe that one needs to have cancer to be grateful, but if one is to endure something so challenging, then we must be able to learn and grow in the process. I am grateful for an easy recovery from surgery, and overall good health, which I know will get me through this marathon. My situation is not unique, but the fact that I am the wife of a public figure has encouraged me to share this journey publicly.

I am proud to say that I have completed round 1 of six rounds of chemotherapy, but that is not all I want to share. I am grateful for the love and support of my husband, Rick, and our children, Jordan, and Samuel. My mom has been a rock of support, as she successfully fought cancer five years ago. My family, friends and co-workers at Creative Clay have been compassionate, understanding, and loving. I could not ask for more, except if you are so inclined, prayers of health, healing, and strength. Here is to what I know will be an amazing 2020; watch for me in an upcoming half marathon. I may be running, walking, or a little of both, but once this marathon is over, there is no stopping me!

The response was overwhelming. The *Times* and local television stations reported portions of my statement verbatim. Instead of creating stress, the announcement generated support from the community. People who commented on my Facebook post promised prayers, sent good wishes, and lauded me for bravery. Everyone who faces a life-threatening health challenge is brave. The difference for me was that I was the spouse of a public figure, which made it newsworthy.

I decided to post from each chemotherapy session. I included a photograph of myself, so that people could see that although I was pale and bald, with no eyelashes or eyebrows, I was fine. I wanted to demystify cancer treatment and hopefully inspire others who might find themselves navigating a cancer diagnosis.

When the doctor in California told me that I likely had stage 4 cancer, I prayed for faith, strength and positivity. I also resolved to help others if I survived. I now use *my* words to help educate medical students and nursing students in the Ovarian Cancer Research Alliance's "Survivors to Students" teaching program. I've joined 200 other "advocate leaders" to represent the Alliance as we lobby members of Congress about the need for funding, access and resources for women with ovarian cancer.

As a political spouse, I know words can hurt. They also heal.

Life's struggles challenge us to find faith. Not only religious faith, but faith in others and in ourselves. Many people have helped me cultivate the inner strength I conjure to survive tough moments.

Political life has afforded me opportunities to connect with people outside my circle of family and friends. Cancer interrupted my path when I least expected it. But it renewed my faith and showed me how to appreciate life like I hadn't in a long time.

Sometimes, people enter our lives with exquisite timing. A Saturday evening walk with our dogs, during the height of the Covid pandemic and the national Black Lives Matter protests, led me to an interaction with a neighbor who provided comfort I didn't know I needed.

After 4 of 6 chemotherapy treatments

— Chapter 21 —

RECOGNIZING HUMANITY

When many of us were quarantined at home during the early months of the Covid-19 pandemic, evening walks provided much-needed interactions with other people. We relied on the ritual of socially distanced conversations with neighbors who also walked their dogs after "Jeopardy."

On Independence Day 2020 St. Pete's traditional downtown waterfront fireworks were canceled. People still set off store-bought fireworks that rumbled throughout the neighborhood and caused a skittish Jake, our career-changed former guide dog in training, to pull Rick toward home five minutes into our evening walk. Jordan and I continued around the lake. I walked Christie, our other Labrador who almost became a guide dog before she was injured. Jordan walked Hannah, our guide dog puppy in training. After Rick put Jake in the house, he walked next door with a bottle of apology wine. That wasn't the brand, but the sentiment.

It was the least we could do for neighbors George on the left and Dennis on the right after that day's 8 a.m. horn-honking wake-up call, when about 20 Black Lives Matters protesters descended on our street to interrupt our Saturday morning ritual of Belgian waffles – blueberry for Rick and me and chocolate chip for Jordan and Samuel.

"No justice, no peace!" they shouted repeatedly as they poured out of their cars with blankets, water bottles and snacks, a party tent, a microphone and an amplifier. Some parked their cars to block people from driving down our street.

They'd made their case for 40 days and nights, in the scorching heat and thunderstorms, to protest the killing of George Floyd, a

Black man, by white police officer Derek Chauvin in Minneapolis. They'd marched through downtown St. Pete on busy Beach Drive NE, through affluent neighborhoods and in front of the police station. That Independence Day, our street was their stage. Neighbors and joggers, walkers and cyclists who passed through the neighborhood were the audience.

They took turns voicing their opposition to what they called unfair and unequal city policies and police procedures. Some of the adults invited the young children to use their tiny voices to speak through the microphone about oppression, justice and hate.

They took breaks from yelling to blast music and snap selfies next to the homemade signs they'd planted in our yard. They seemed unaware that Rick understood their cause and was striving to balance supporting their right to free speech while advocating for the city's police officers. They were in front of our house for one reason: They had nine actions they wanted the city to take. St. Pete had already addressed eight of them. The ninth was for Rick to reduce the amount of money the city budget allocated to police.

Spencer "Thirteen" Cook, a protest leader, told the *Tampa Bay Times* that this would be the first of many times protesters would come to our house. "We are occupying his neighborhood the same way our neighborhoods are occupied," Cook said, according to the paper. "The same way we are uncomfortable, they need to be uncomfortable. The ship is sinking, and everyone should be uncomfortable."

(In fact, protesters returned to our house a week later for another demonstration. That led to the arrest of a woman and a child, who police said was under the age of 12, who sat in the middle of the street blocking traffic. The *Times* said that prompted this disavowal on the Facebook page of the protest group: "Just for the record BLACK leadership was not in support of going to the mayor's house this morning. That behavior is unacceptable.")

St. Pete hadn't experienced the violence, looting and vandalism that other U.S. cities had seen after the murder of Floyd, but the protesters still marched and chanted through megaphones to advocate for their cause. Days earlier, when some of the protesters stationed outside the police station asked Rick and police Chief Anthony Holloway to take a knee with them, they both did. Still, some of the protestors didn't believe Rick was supportive enough.

No city is perfect, but Rick and his team had worked hard to improve racial equity. His administration pursued affordable housing, supported Black businesses, and worked to improve equity in the ranks of the police department.

Shortly after the protesters arrived that morning, Jordan drew the blackout drapes in her bedroom, which was in the front of the house. After one of the protesters waved to us through the sheer white curtains in our dining room, we closed the heavier, brown acetate panels so no one could see inside. I closed the wood blinds in our home office, sat on the Formica counter, and peeked through the slats. The crepe myrtle tree in our front yard had grown large enough in the 11 years that it shaded the office window. We could see out, but no one could see in. Rick cautioned me to not let the protesters see me, but they weren't focused on the windows. They fixated on our front door, hoping Rick would open it, walk outside and address the crowd. Police officers stationed in the neighborhood in unmarked cars advised Rick not to go outside.

As they had done each night during their marches, the protesters broadcast from our home on Facebook Live. Soon, a *Times* reporter arrived. Friends who saw protesters' social media posts offered to bring food or pick us up in the alley. I assured them we were safe. We didn't try to silence Jake's barks. If the protesters thought we weren't home, maybe they would leave.

Frustrated with Rick's refusal to come out, they sent children to our front door 14 times to ring the doorbell. By the fourth hour, Jake stopped barking.

After five hours, the protesters packed up their tent, signs and snacks, and left.

We opened the drapes and blinds to see an empty street and clean lawn. A family of ducks crossed the street. It was as if nothing happened.

Samuel went to golf practice. Jordan researched graduate schools and did training drills with Hannah. Rick and I went to Best Buy to shop the holiday sales on appliances.

I thought we all did a good job at pivoting that day. Jordan and Samuel showed us that they had the thick skin that took me years to attain after Rick entered politics in 1999.

It wasn't until our regular evening walk with our dogs and the conversation with a stranger that I realized that sometimes thick skin cracks.

While Rick talked with George on his front stoop, Jordan and I continued walking Christie and Hannah. I don't always remember the neighbors' names, but we know the dogs. Fred the yellow Labrador walks without a leash, always obeying his master, Harold. Tigger the black papillon pulls the retractable leash several feet in front of his master, an 87-year-old retired preacher. Bear the rescue boxer is timid, so he and Christie had greeted each other from a distance long before Covid.

When an unfamiliar woman who was walking her mixed-breed dog said hello from a distance, Jordan and I waved and went one way, while she went another.

Halfway around the lake, I saw the woman and her dog walk up to our front door. Just like earlier that day, there would be yelling. This time it was me.

"Honey! Honey!" I called to Rick as I pulled Christie around the lake. "Someone is coming to our house."

I walked faster with Christie.

"She's walking up to our door!" I yelled.

Rick and George didn't hear me.

"Honey!" I yelled again. My throat was sore by now.

My heart was pounding. Throughout the afternoon, a few of the protesters had driven by our house, possibly hoping to catch Rick outside. I thought this woman might be one of them.

"Can I help you with something?" I asked her. She stopped knocking on our door and walked toward me. She wasn't wearing a mask, so I backed up to make space between us. Every time I backed up, she moved toward me. I saw tears.

"I know I can't, but I just want to give you a hug," she said.

Now she was crying. My shoulders relaxed, and I sighed a breath that I could tell had been pent up all day. I loosened my grip on Christie's leash, so she could say hello to the woman's dog. The woman told me she had to have her other dog euthanized hours earlier. Then she said, "I just want to thank your husband for what he is doing to keep us safe." She had heard about the protesters earlier that day. She was worried about us.

Fear turned to compassion for this grieving woman who walked six blocks to deliver a heartfelt message.

"I feel so bad for your family," she said.

When Rick was elected mayor in 2013, life changed overnight. Unfamiliar cars sometimes drove slowly by our house. They would circle the lake a few times, then sit in their cars near our house sometimes for up to 30 minutes. Sometimes, people took photos of our home. When asked, one woman told me she liked the brick on the square columns on our front porch. Another time, someone complimented the color of our home.

Sometimes, gawkers drove away quickly after seeing me walk out the front door with one of our dogs. I suspected they were scoping our house because of something Rick had said or done. If a police car was stationed outside our home for several days, it was usually in response to threats made toward Rick.

Protesters may have inconvenienced our idyllic Saturday morning, but the yelling, music and doorbell ringing was tolerable compared to the vandalism and graffiti other U.S. mayors dealt with after the killing of Floyd.

People often describe me as calm and steady. When people ask how I survive political life, I tell them I have had two decades of practice. After the protesters spent five hours camped out in front of our home, I understood the impact of political discord, an incurable virus, and unending racism. I also understood how easy it was for fear to overtake our emotions.

I almost mistook an act of humanity as an invasion of privacy. In her grief at losing her dog earlier that day, a woman walked six blocks to tell us she was sorry for the disruption outside our home.

I was embarrassed that fear led me to think that she was there to cause trouble. Even an experienced, thick-skinned political spouse can succumb to fear. I thought I had pushed the morning's events out of my mind. My reaction showed that I had only suppressed the stress. I was no different than the millions of people affected by the events of 2020. My status as the mayor's wife didn't give me immunity from negativity.

When protesters disrupted our quiet Saturday morning, I told myself it was part of the job. I never expected it to affect me. After two decades as a political spouse, I knew how to steel myself to survive political campaigns. I'd run that marathon eight times. I'd seen Rick's name in the media and on television hundreds of times, and I learned how not to let a negative story ruin my day.

I thrived whether Rick was working in St. Pete or another state. I was no longer lonely when he was gone, like I was near the beginning of his political career when he was a state legislator living in Tallahassee for 60 days during the annual session.

Independence Day 2020 reminded me that to survive political life I must also be gentle with myself. Not every stranger who comes to your home is there for a dubious reason. The sad but compassionate woman who only wanted to thank Rick for his service and offer our family emotional support reinforced my belief in the goodness of others.

The events of that day reminded me to remember to keep the faith, a practice I have learned from several unexpected sources during my time as a political spouse.

— Chapter 22 —

HAVE A LITTLE FAITH

Eddie Pelham had been incarcerated for 25 years for crimes that began when he was only 14. Someone who had spent most of his life in prison might be short on faith. Not Eddie. After leaving prison, he became an ordained minister and started Moving Forward with a Purpose, Inc., a nonprofit program for at-risk youth. He wanted to make life better for others.

Eddie's work focuses on at-risk youth aged 7 to 24 who might easily take the wrong path if not guided by caring adults. He wants to make the community better for these youths and others who live in low-income neighborhoods just south of St. Petersburg's Central Avenue.

It was Eddie's faith that guided his life's work. A faith that was rooted in his belief in the power of prayer, a lesson he learned from his grandmother, Beullah Pelham.

When Rick first ran for mayor in 2013, many did not know the lawyer and former City Council member and state House representative.

Eddie was one of the first volunteers who believed in Rick's vision for a more inclusive and equitable city. Eddie could've been bitter toward a system that dealt with him sternly, but he had faith that if Rick were elected mayor, life would improve for many who'd been overlooked.

Yet it wasn't until four years after I met Eddie that I would see his faith in action.

We'd arrived at Greater Mt. Zion A.M.E. Church for another debate between candidates for the 2017 mayoral election. Being at a church didn't guarantee that we wouldn't experience the chaos that had erupted two days earlier at the Hilton St. Petersburg Bayfront, when police had to break up the raucous debate.

Eddie greeted our family when we arrived at the church. He is always quick with a hug, and it was comforting to feel his support among people filing in who were obviously supporting Rick's opponents. It was time to go in, but Eddie stopped us, took our hands, and started to pray. Rick, Jordan, Samuel, campaign manager Jacob Smith and I held hands with Eddie leading a prayer of peace. He prayed for God to watch over Rick and our family. Eddie reminded us that this campaign, like much in life, was in God's hands.

The summer of 2017 would be an education in how we can summon faith when things sometime seem hopeless. There were moments I wasn't sure whether Rick would be reelected. When our family was invited to attend several predominantly Black churches that summer, we experienced an unconditional love that had nothing to do with who the congregants supported for mayor.

A few weeks earlier, in the middle of the Sunday service at Greater Mt. Zion A.M.E., Pastor Clarence Williams called Rick, Jordan, Samuel and me to kneel at the altar. We folded our hands, and we bowed our heads and listened to Pastor Williams talk about the mayor's race. Then, we felt the soft touch of hands on our shoulders from four congregants who emerged from the back of the church. We kept our heads down while Pastor Williams asked the congregants to pray for our family, specifically Rick, as the mayor's race continued through the summer. He implored the congregation to pray for our family the way they prayed for Rick Baker's family the week before.

Pastor Williams' words reminded me that we all need prayers, even our opponents. I took it as a personal challenge to keep the faith, even when the campaign grew darkly vitriolic and negative.

My prayer requests had always been basic. I prayed for things like good health and safety for our family. I thought I was asking for too much to pray for Rick to win the election. So, I prayed for faith, an action that Merriam-Webster defines as the ability to believe in something for which there is no proof. No matter the results, I believed God had our backs.

Campaigning at predominantly white churches is usually verboten. In the Black community, it's customary for candidates to make the rounds on the Sunday that Communion is offered – a day that often garners the highest attendance.

At Mt. Zion Progressive Missionary Baptist Church, Pastor Louis Murphy Sr. invited us to his office before services. We talked about the effect politicians in Tallahassee and Washington, D.C., have on local communities. Rick's opponents and some in the media argued that Rick was wrong to tie his most formidable opponent — Baker — to fellow Republican Donald Trump because the president's policies and behavior had nothing to do with St. Petersburg.

Rick was adamant that what politicians in Tallahassee and Washington did directly affect the people he was elected to serve. Pastor Murphy asked me if I agreed. I told him I did, and that I supported Rick's criticism of the Trump policies that harmed immigrants, Black and brown people, and members of the LGBTQ community. Murphy then asked how I was handling the campaigning. As I began to answer, I heard the choir singing as they welcomed church goers. They sang a message I'd never heard. Over and over, they praised God for waking them up that morning.

None of what I'd learned as a Catholic taught me to start each day by thanking God that I had awakened.

This simple yet profound act gave me new perspective on life in the political spotlight. Rick's job as a politician had been center stage for almost 20 years. I often talked about the bubble of politics Rick lived in when he was a state representative in Tallahassee. That morning in Pastor Murphy's office I realized I'd sequestered myself in my own political bubble. I had been so consumed with Rick's reelection campaign and all the negativity and stress that ensued that I'd neglected to be grateful for waking up each day.

That morning, I was gifted with a renewed faith that wasn't borne from religions, but from a belief that we would make it through this tumultuous campaign. Every time we attended a Black church that summer, we were welcomed with open arms and hugs. I looked forward to walking into the rousing music and warm embraces. Congregants offered us their Bibles so we could follow along with that week's passages. Samuel says I'm stoic, but I clapped and swayed to the music. It felt good to be among people who believed so mightily that it poured out in their words and movements. Pastor Murphy's choir reminded me how uplifted I felt when I attended a full Gospel church in Washington, D.C., with my church youth group when I was 15.

I continued to pray for faith as we headed into the homestretch of the campaign. I looked for tools that I could use that connected me with God and gave me the same feeling of inspiration I felt when we attended the Black churches.

I started every morning with a walk through our neighborhood. During those walks, I often called my mom or my brother. Sometimes, I made mental notes of the day's tasks. The walks set the tone for the day; if I couldn't get to the gym, at least I'd gotten a little exercise.

As we neared election day, my morning walks became a meditation. I listened to the birds, noticed the flowers and trees, and admired the sunrise. I added music to my walks.

"Whenever God Shines His Light," by Van Morrison, reminded me that God opens our eyes so that we can see. Morrison sings that "in the darkest night... everything's going to be alright" and that "if you live the life you love, you get the blessing from above."

I played it over and over as my pace quickened. After the campaign was over, I returned to that song when I needed faith.

Some say that our experiences prepare us for the future, and that there are lessons in everything we do.

I now know that the experience of the 2017 mayoral campaign and the people who entered my life because of it, prepared me for the cancer diagnosis I would receive less than two years later. I started to remember to thank God for waking me up each day. Cancer is a jolting reminder that each day is not promised.

Rick entered politics on a whim. We had nothing to lose, but we must've had faith to think he could win as an unknown political neophyte. Throughout the years, we upped the ante. Six years on the City Council led to six years in the state House, then eight years as mayor. We raised our children in the public eye. We celebrated good times and grieved when our home burned, and our pets died. Through it all, we kept the faith.

Many people we might have never met came into our lives because of politics. I might never have known about Eddie's struggles and triumphs if Rick hadn't run for mayor. I am almost certain we wouldn't have attended a dozen Black churches where we met people of different faiths who trusted my husband to lead their city and who opened their arms to invite us to worship.

Most of the people I've met because of Rick's job care as much as he does about making life better for others. Although it was at first an unlikely, if not accidental role, life as a political spouse and first lady of St. Pete has taught me about the goodness of most people. During a campaign, I am always humbled when someone spends free time volunteering for Rick. I continue to be awed that people give their hard-earned money and precious time to support his quest for public office. It's the same feeling I had when people we didn't know put their hands gently on our shoulders as we knelt in prayer. Politics can make you feel alone, but that simple gesture, and Eddie's impromptu prayer, reminded me we are never alone.

Lessons of faith sometimes come from unlikely sources, and when we least expect them. But somehow, they always arrive exactly when we need them. And that's no accident.

EPILOGUE

Andy Warhol's 1968 proclamation that, "In the future, everyone will be world-famous for *15 minutes*" is an oft-heard cliché for a status attained by few. Being a political spouse doesn't render one famous, but the special experiences and privileges I've enjoyed over the last 22 years came only *because* I was a political spouse.

If you've read this far, then you know I never sought the spotlight. I landed there because Rick said yes to running for the City Council in January 1999. Looking back, it seemed as if our decision for Rick to seek political office was made on a whim, but the impact of that decision has dictated the course of most of our married life and virtually the entire lives of our kids.

Jordan was just 18 months old when Rick lost that first election. Samuel was just 7 weeks old when he made it known loud and clear that he wasn't in the mood for politics. We were at City Hall for the swearing in of newly elected council members. When it was Rick's turn, he cradled Samuel in the crook of his left arm, his right hand on the Torah. Samuel cried the entire time, then abruptly stopped when the ceremony ended.

Ten years later, when Rick was elected mayor, Samuel stood next to Rick on stage. This time, no tears. Only cheers.

Some spouses would trade places with me in a minute, on the assumption that as a political couple, our social lives are richer, the perks are bountiful and that somehow life is easier. Other people would leave skid marks at the first mention of their spouse running for office.

I've learned to embrace the experiences that were a byproduct of political life as opportunities. They've brought me more than that singular "15 minutes of fame" that Warhol spoke about.

Not many couples can say they spent Valentine's Day on the set of a nationally televised Hallmark movie. With one day's notice, I pulled a formal gown from my closet and Rick brushed off his tuxedo so we could join producers, directors and actors at the St. Petersburg Museum of Fine Arts.

Our scene was set in the museum's garden, and we were there with other gala guests awaiting the arrival of the fictional female mayor. We toasted with fake champagne goblets, mouthed fake party conversation, and made sure not to bite into the waxed hors d'oeuvres.

On the set of True Love Blooms, *Museum of Fine Arts, St. Pete - 2019*

I don't watch Hallmark movies, but I appreciate their value in transporting the viewer to an idyllic, esoteric place where imperfect circumstances lead to beautiful conclusions. You could say that's how politics can be.

Things always end up working out, even when unplanned. When we attended the screening of *True Love Blooms* when it premiered in April 2019, we made sure not to blink and risk missing our cameo.

Years earlier, we had a brush with fame when Rick was on the City Council and was asked to present a key to the city to Ringo Starr. After Rick gave Ringo the key, I told the former Beatle how

Jordan fiercely kicked me in utero during his 1997 concert, signaling she was destined to become an Irish step dancer.

Afterward, I asked Rick, "So, what's cooler? Meeting President Clinton or Ringo Starr?"

We had stood in many rope lines and had our photos taken countless times, but never had we met a Beatle.

Ringo wouldn't be the last rock star I'd meet before Rick's tenure on the council ended. Rick and I were dancing to "Brick House" at the Honda Grand Prix welcome party in 2006 when council member Bill Foster called us over for a photo with Kiss front man Gene Simmons, who was in St. Pete to serve as grand marshal of the race.

I was the only female in the group, and Simmons motioned for me to stand in front of him. I smiled through the tight bear hug that left the herniated disc in my neck smarting for a few hours.

Our introduction to the original Parrot Head was much tamer. By now, Rick was serving his third term in the state House. It was Friday, April 16, 2011. Rick was on his way home from Tallahassee. He called to tell me to meet him at the Florida Amphitheatre at 3 p.m. He had a proclamation to deliver to Jimmy Buffett. Samuel was already wearing his "Save the Manatees" shirt, very apropos since Rick was presenting the proclamation to honor Buffett's impact on Florida and his work on manatee conservation.

Rick, Jordan, Samuel and I, and our second guide dog puppy in training, Elvis, sat in the empty amphitheater during the band's rehearsal and listened to several renditions of "Floridays." Later, a barefoot Buffett posed for a photo with us, laughed when Elvis licked his shorts, then gave us a backstage tour.

A few of the other guide dog puppies we've raised for Southeastern Guide Dogs have also enjoyed some fame. Jim, the first pup we raised, joined Rick on the House floor when he advocated for a bill to strengthen Florida's laws about service animals. Speaker Dean Cannon killed the bill, but hundreds of people on the floor and in the gallery heard about the importance of service animals.

Our sixth pup in training was aptly named Sunshine. We picked her up the day after the 2014 Mayoral Ball, just over a week after Rick took office as mayor. She was "The First Pup of St. Pete." Her Facebook page kept followers abreast of her training and was full of photos from the events she attended, such as the annual Sunrise Sale in downtown St. Pete.

City photographers enjoyed photographing Sunshine amid her stash of toys in Rick's office. After Sunshine was matched with a visually impaired woman in Minneapolis, we welcomed Christie, whom *Creative Loafing* named "Best Mayoral Dog" in its annual "Best of the Bay" conteSt.

Rick was probably one of the only mayors whose family raised guide dog puppies, something we started in 2009 when Jordan requested to raise a pup for her bat mitzvah service project. When Rick became mayor, I was occasionally asked to speak about our work with Southeastern Guide Dogs. Local news stations came to our home to interview me, and a few local magazines did features on us and the pups.

We also fundraised for the organization. One night, many of the volunteers, and our family and friends, took over Hamburger Mary's for Drag Queen Bingo. A portion of the proceeds from the evening would be donated to Southeastern Guide Dogs. Rick arrived that evening as I was trying to fill my Bingo card so I could yell the winning phrase, "It's on, bitches!"

I've always thought Rick is handsome, but I was still surprised when the queens stopped the game and exclaimed, "It's the hot mayor!" When he sat down next to me, I was crowned his "skinny bitch." This went on for the rest of the night. "It's the hot mayor and the skinny bitch!" the queens yelled. They loved Rick for his longtime support of the LGBTQ community. When they called us up to the stage, the crowd roared while we were photographed arm in arm with the towering queens.

Most of the time, it's been Rick on stage while the kids and I watch from the audience. The four of us have only shared the stage four times – both times when he was elected mayor and when he was sworn in.

Jordan had been an Irish step dancer for 11 years by the time Rick was invited to introduce her and other dancers before they performed with the Florida Orchestra at the Mahaffey Theater.

I watched as the dancers' crystal-covered dresses glistened as they stood with Rick. The bright lights couldn't hide Rick's beaming pride as he shared the stage with his daughter.

A stage can also be a venue for advocacy. Elected office comes with a built-in platform that some like to call a bully pulpit. As mayor, Rick felt he had a responsibility to use his platform as the city's leader when people and groups were mistreated.

On the second night of Hanukkah in 2015, 21 words tweeted by Rick during our family celebration earned him his first appearance on MSNBC the day after we attended the White House holiday party:

"I am hereby barring Donald Trump from entering St. Petersburg until we fully understand the dangerous threat posed by all Trumps."

Rick's tweet was a response to presidential candidate Trump's statement on the supposed dangers of allowing Muslims into the United States. Rick's statement was liked 19,300 times, retweeted 15,800 times, and generated more than 2,000 comments.

Jordan, Samuel and I sat in a closet-sized room and watched Rick answer MSNBC anchor Richard Lui's questions from the New York City studio. A few minutes later a staffer retrieved us and led us to the set. We took turns sitting at the anchor desk.

It was a quiet Saturday on the set. Just the four of us, a producer and a cameraman. After the interview, the producer flipped on the lights to reveal *Meet the Press* moderator Chuck Todd's set. They let us spend as much time as we wanted checking out the memorabilia, awards, bumper stickers, including one from the 1960 Kennedy/Johnson campaign, and a framed collection of Todd's press badges.

The reaction to the tweet heard 'round the world surprised all of us, but advocacy was typical of Rick's governing style. His record of elevating and advocating those in marginalized groups is a hallmark of his tenure of public service.

Rick was the only City Council member to sign St. Petersburg's first Pride Proclamation in 2003. In the middle of his 2013 reelection campaign, then-Mayor Bill Foster signed the proclamation — six days after first refusing to sign it. As mayor, Rick went further to support the LGBTQ community. In 2014, his first year as mayor, Rick raised the rainbow flag at City Hall during Pride Month. He raised it every year throughout his eight-year tenure. Our family walked in the Pride parade, the largest in the Southeastern United States. He danced down the street, zigzagging across the street to fist bump, high five and hug parade participants and watchers.

People were grateful that St. Pete was becoming more inclusive. In response to how Muslims were treated in other U.S. cities, Rick hosted the city's first iftar dinner in 2017. His message that St. Pete would not tolerate the mistreatment of others because of their faith was heard loud and clear by the 800 people at the dinner.

It was our family's introduction to Ramadan. As the room cleared after the dinner ended, families came up to Rick to have their photos taken with him.

As a Catholic mother raising Jewish children, I know that similarities exist among many religions. We are stronger as a community when we focus on similarities and respect differences. In political life, I've tried to see others as people, regardless of religion, political affiliation, or sexual orientation.

A few times, knowing that I was approaching something new made me nervous. When Rick and I traveled to Morocco with five mayors, their spouses and staff, I knew only one other person in the bipartisan delegation: Orlando Mayor Buddy Dyer, whom I'd met once when we walked across the Golden Gate Bridge at sunrise during the 2015 U.S. Conference of Mayors.

Our Morocco group met at Dulles Airport in Washington, D.C. We got to know the people we'd spend the next five days with over drinks and snacks in the lounge while we waited to board our flight to Rabat, the capital of Morocco. By the time we landed, we were comfortable enough with each other to greet the morning with bed head and groggy eyes.

For five days, we traveled from Rabat to Casablanca, then Marrakesh. We bonded while tasting pigeon for the first time and exploring Kasbah of the Udayas, where bright blue doors pop off the background of the white houses.

When Rick told me about the opportunity to travel to Morocco, I searched for guidelines on the protocol regarding head coverings and modest dress codes. I included scarfs to match every outfit. I wondered whether women were afforded the same equality we enjoy in the United States. We visited the Mohammed VI Institute for the Training of Imams, Morchidines and Morchidates in Rabat, the only Imam that trains men *and* women to become spiritual guides. A few days later, we talked with women students at a university outside Marrakesh that trained many women in STEM careers. I saw how the country was truly taking steps to promote gender equality.

Throughout the trip, we used WhatsApp to communicate with our travel mates. Three years later, 14 of us still regularly message each other for birthdays and well wishes for accolades.

Many of the experiences I've had because of Rick's political career are the subjects for the stories we retell our family and friends. In a business fraught with vitriol and, lately, vulgarity, I cherish the once-in-a-lifetime moments afforded to me only because enough people believed in Rick and decided to elect him seven times.

I can't possibly encapsulate two decades as a political spouse into one chapter or even one book. I'm a self-described unlikely political spouse, and an accidental first lady. When I reflect on public life, I'm grateful.

I can't imagine what life would've looked like if Rick hadn't said yes to running for the City Council in January 1999. A movie set, backstage at a concert or on another continent: I've lived bucket-list experiences. Some might say the memorable moments we've had are a fair exchange for the occasional downside of public service. I don't see it like that.

We don't know what's next for Rick's political career. That's okay. Our faith has seen us through tragedy and frightening times that showed us that you can always rebound, rebuild and make new memories. Faith has taught me that uncertainty can lead to joy. My life is richer because of the *people* that politics placed before me. Politics or no politics, I'm certain there will be new memories and new chapters. I just must remember to always keep the faith.

ACKNOWLEDGMENTS

It wasn't until Rick's 2017 reelection campaign that people started asking me, "How do you do this?" I'd logged 18 years as a political spouse where it was Rick who fielded questions from interested constituents, friends and family. He was the focus while I supported him from the sidelines.

The 2017 St. Pete mayoral race was one of the most vitriolic and divisive political campaigns in the city's history. People who didn't usually pay much heed to local politics were caught up in the battle of the Rick's: my husband versus the former two-term mayor who tried to make sure Rick never won a second term as mayor.

Because many were emotionally invested in the outcome of the race, I believe it's why they started to think about the people behind the politician, particularly the spouse or partner.

Toward the end of the campaign, then often after Rick won re-election, I was asked, "How do you do this?" I replied with a stock answer: "Rick loves his job in politics and serving the people who call St. Pete home. We focus on family and what is most important. We know who our true friends are, and we never, ever take one moment of this privileged life for granted."

My reply satisfied most, but my close friends and family knew the stories that included stress, angst, joy and elation. After the dust settled on that victorious reelection campaign, I began to assess my personal and professional life. Throughout the previous seven campaigns, no one asked what life as a political spouse was like for me. No one seemed to care or even know what I did for a living. People didn't seem interested in the politician's partner. I was content with that. Politics is a very public job, but in the end, it was Rick's job. I didn't expect to answer others' questions about how his job impacted my life.

In January 2018, as Rick was settling into his second term as St. Petersburg's mayor, I accepted an invitation to coffee from Melanie Lenz, chief development officer for the Tampa Bay Rays. We'd known each other for several years from our board service on the Heart Gallery of Pinellas & Pasco. Over coffee at Craft Kafe, she asked THE QUESTION: "How do you do this?"

One-on-one, and woman-to-woman, I gave more than my stock answer. I honestly told her how the recent campaign had upended our lives for six months.

Intrigued, she said, "You should write a book."

Melanie planted the seed, and after we hugged goodbye, I texted Rick about the idea of a book. As he has always done throughout our 30 years together, he enthusiastically supported me.

Still, I wondered if my stories would resonate with others. Susan Sheppard Fekete, a childhood friend who was in the middle of publishing her own memoir told me, "If it's inside of you, then you need to share it."

Over the next seven months, more people suggested I write a book. When I asked the opinion of our media consultant, John Rowley, he said, "Do it!"

After I wrote a few chapters, I enlisted my friend, Jeff Klinkenberg. Jeff and I had worked together at the *St. Petersburg Times*, now *Tampa Bay Times*. A celebrated author of eight books, he shared his wisdom of writing and the publishing industry.

I carried Jeff's "show, don't tell" advice with me throughout this process.

Local author Lori Roy and I met when our daughters were in the same kindergarten class. An award-winning author, I hesitated for months to share my book idea and writing with her. Lori's thoughtful feedback was like attending a masterclass on writing. When she described my writing as "almost poetic in spots," I committed to finishing the book.

Trusted friends Jennifer Corbett and Diana Calandra read early chapters. My sister-in-law, Nancy Kriseman, herself an author, provided invaluable inspiration from her unique point of view. Aunt Frances Kennedy served as family historian and ensured my account of our family's history was accurate.

Political pros Jason Bennett and Reiny Cohen graciously spent a couple of hours with me on a Friday morning in 2019 while I talked about this project on their podcast, "Election University."

After a nine-month hiatus from writing after my cancer diagnosis and subsequent chemotherapy and radiation, I resumed sending pitches and queries to publishing companies big and small. Many nice rejections included the similar refrain. My story was interesting. I was a good writer, but I didn't have enough of a platform and following. I considered self-publishing, then ran quickly away from a hybrid publisher who wanted to charge way too much to sell me services I didn't need as a requirement for publishing.

Finally, I got up the nerve to call local writing expert and teacher Roy Peter Clark. When I told him I'd written about 60,000 words, he said, "Congratulations, you're an author."

Those four words made me believe this was worth publishing. I'm grateful for Roy who connected me with St. Petersburg Press. Amy Cianci and Joe Hamilton were patient with this first-time author. They answered the same questions more than twice and shepherded me through this new and daunting process.

Rick has always said that so much of what happens to us in life is about relationships. He's right. When I needed an editor, an email from Roy arrived, suggesting a former colleague from the *St. Petersburg Times*. I hadn't seen Rob Hooker since 1998, but I knew he was a gifted editor and reporter who had worked for the *Times* for more than 40 years. Retired and willing to work with a novice author, Rob's wisdom and expertise propelled me to the finish line.

Just because the book was finished didn't mean it was done. Longtime friends Jean Galanos and Kevin King combed through every word, phrase and paragraph to make sure Rob and I didn't miss anything. Their keen attention to detail was invaluable.

The photographic talent of City of St. Petersburg staffers Michael and Maria Flanagan have given our family many cherished photos, a few that are in this book.

It goes without saying that the person I love and trust the most in this world was my biggest cheerleader. Rick patiently and thoroughly read every version of every chapter. Knowing he was in my corner and that he believed in me, and the book, kept me writing. I'm grateful that we have a relationship borne of honesty. The ability to have Rick's eye and opinion was a gift.

Our children, Jordan and Samuel, were so supportive during

my writing sessions, which required solitude and quiet. I hope I've made you proud.

To the people of St. Petersburg and the surrounding areas, thank you. Your confidence in my husband's ability to advocate and represent you is what provided this amazing, if not accidental, political life. It has been my pleasure and honor to know many of you and learn from you. You have taught me much about the love of cities and communities.

To the readers of this book: Thank you for taking the time to support a new author. Thank you for spending time with me through my stories. I hope they resonate with you. I hope you see yourself in some of my experiences, even if you aren't a first lady or political spouse.

↑ *Kriseman Family, St. Petersburg, Florida, 2004*

↑ *March for Our Lives, St. Petersburg, Florida, March 2018*

↑ *Jordan and Samuel Kriseman, Election Night, November 5, 2013, NOVA 535, St. Petersburg, Florida*

↑ *Thanksgiving with paternal grand-parents Joseph and Anne Nicolosi, St. Petersburg, Florida – 1981*

↑ *Opening day at the new St. Pete Pier, St. Petersburg, Florida, July 6, 2020*

↑ *With Kiss front man Gene Simmons, St. Petersburg Grand Prix welcome party – 2005*

↑ *Sunshine, the First Puppy of St. Pete and the 6th Southeastern Guide Dogs puppy in training raised by the Kriseman Family, St. Petersburg City Hall – 2014*

↑ *Kriseman family in North Carolina, January 2007*

↑ *Election appreciation sign waving, St. Petersburg, Florida, November 2017*

↑ *Family Christmas card, St. Petersburg, Florida – 1971*

↑ *With President Joe Biden, American Promise Tour, Mahaffey Theater, St. Petersburg, Florida, June 2018*

↑ *With Ringo Starr, Mahaffey Theater, St. Petersburg, Florida – 2005*

↑ *With Jimmy Buffett, Florida Amphitheater, Tampa, Florida, 2011. Pictured with the Kriseman family is Kevin King, senior legislative assistant*

↑ *With former Gov. Charlie Crist, bill signing, St. Petersburg, Florida, 2007*

ABOUT THE AUTHOR

Kerry Kriseman is a St. Petersburg native. She was born in St. Anthony's Hospital, the same hospital where her grandmother was an OB/GYN nurse and where her daughter was born. Kerry is a graduate of University of South Florida with a B.A. in Mass Communications/Broadcasting.

Her professional career spans 30 years with a 10-year stint in between, raising her two children (Jordan, 23, and Samuel, 18), volunteering in the community and serving on multiple non-profit boards.

Kerry worked in print media for the *St. Petersburg Times* (now *Tampa Bay Times*) in various positions in the Newsroom and Marketing Department. When her youngest child Samuel began Kindergarten in 2008, Kerry joined Creative Clay as the public relations manager. The non-profit creates equality through art with programs for individuals with neuro-differences.

Kerry and her family are volunteer puppy raisers for Southeastern Guide Dogs. They are now raising their 12th guide dog puppy in training, Irwin. Five of the pups raised are working guides. One is a Gold Star Family Dog. Two are beloved family pets. Another was designated a Southeastern Guide Dog Ambassador, the remaining two are Kriseman family pets.

Despite its challenges, Kerry has enjoyed being a political spouse to her husband throughout his 22-year political career. For the past seven years, she has enjoyed being an "accidental first lady" of St. Petersburg, Florida. Historical dramas, traveling, scratch cooking, drinking wine, daily walks, and long bike rides on the Pinellas Trail fill any free time.